KIDDING AROUND

Chicago

A YOUNG PERSON'S GUIDE

SECOND EDITION

LAUREN DAVIS

ILLUSTRATED BY SALLY BLAKEMORE

John Muir Publications
Santa Fe, New Mexico

*For Aaron and Peter Lazar,
A.B. Wilson, Max Coll,
C. and D. Hall*

*Special thanks to Jamie and
Stuart Abelson, Jan and
Don Barliant, Larry Hildes,
Daktahmo Nelligan,
Andrew Patner, Marion
Rosenbluth, and SL*

John Muir Publications, P.O. Box 613, Santa Fe, NM 87504

© 1990, 1993 by Lauren Davis
Illustrations © 1990, 1993 by Sally Blakemore
Cover © 1990, 1993 by John Muir Publications
All rights reserved. Published 1990
Printed in the United States of America

Second edition. Third printing August 1995.

Library of Congress Cataloging-in-Publication Data
Davis, Lauren, 1955-
    Kidding around Chicago: a young person's guide /
Lauren Davis; illustrated by Sally Blakemore.—2nd ed.
        p.   cm.
    Includes index.
    Summary: Provides historical and cultural information
as well as a guide to the sights of Chicago and its suburbs.
    ISBN 1-56261-094-5
    1. Chicago (Ill.)—Guidebooks—Juvenile literature.
    2. Children—Travel—Illinois—Chicago—Guidebooks—
Juvenile literature. [1. Chicago (Ill.)—Guides.]
    I. Blakemore, Sally, ill. II. Title.
    F548.18.D38 1993
    917.7311'0443—dc20   92-41214
                                                      CIP
                                                      AC

Cover photo: John G. Shedd Aquarium/Edward Lines, Jr.
Typeface: Utopia
Typography: Ken Wilson
Printer: Bookcrafters

Distributed to the book trade by
Publishers Group West
Emeryville, California

Distributed to the education market by
Wright Group Publishing, Inc.
19201 120th Avenue N.E.
Bothell, WA 98011-9512

*Buckingham Fountain is
280 feet across at the bottom, spouts water 135 feet
into the air, and contains
1,500,000 gallons of water.*

Contents

To remember everything you see, hear, feel, and taste while traveling, bring alone a journal. Write in it. Draw pictures. Press flowers between the pages. Take along a tape recorder. Talk into it and interview the people you meet.

1. Why the Windy City?

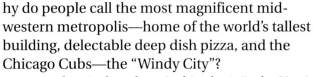

hy do people call the most magnificent midwestern metropolis—home of the world's tallest building, delectable deep dish pizza, and the Chicago Cubs—the "Windy City"?

Rumor has it that the wind in the Windy City is strong enough to knock folks off the sidewalks. While it's true that when an easterly "Hawk" kicks up you'll grab your hat and the nearest lamppost, Chicago does not get its nickname from stormy weather. The nickname comes from a New York reporter who claimed Chicagoans were full of "wind" because they bragged so about their city's attributes while they were bidding to become hosts for the 1893 World's Fair. The name stuck. Residents and outsiders alike began referring to Chicago as the "Windy City."

Chicagoans still love to boast about the city's beginnings when it was a marshy, smelly swampland called *che-cau-gua* (which means something like "great," "wild onion," or "skunk cabbage," depending on who you talk to) by the area's earliest residents, Native Americans.

The first non-Indian settlers in the area were French explorers and fur trappers who arrived in the 1600s, followed by Chicago's first recorded permanent resident, Jean Baptiste Point Du Sable, a black man who researchers say may have been from Santo Domingo.

Chicago quickly became the main link connecting the eastern and western parts of the United States. The area was also situated along a major route of waterways joining Canada with New Orleans and the Gulf of Mexico. For this reason, the place that was once a murky marsh quickly grew from being a small settlement of only 200 residents in 1831 to a hustling bustling town of over 4,000 people by 1837.

In the 1850s, thousands of miles of railroad were built joining Chicago with other major U.S. cities. The Windy City soon became the central hub of shipping and trade for the entire nation. People came from all over the country to work on the expanding railways. They also came from around the globe—from Germany, Ireland, Sweden, Eastern Europe, Italy, Greece, and Africa—to find opportunity. The city, now with a population of over 3 million, has more recently become home to Arab, Mexican, Chinese, Vietnamese, West African, and East Indian immigrants, many of whom have settled in the Windy City's ethnic neighborhoods. This mix of language and culture makes the city a place Chicagoans are proud of.

Walk through a few of Chicago's neighborhoods, and in the markets you'll see barrels of

Marshall Field & Company's flagship store on the State Street Mall in Chicago

Photo courtesy of Ron Schramm/Chicago Office of Tourism

"Hawk" refers to the cold slicing wind that whips out of the Chicago winter sky. The term became popular after Chicago rhythm and blues singer Lou Rawls sang about the hawk in his song, "Dead End Street."

Chicago is often called the "Second City" because it was once second in size after New York, but it has actually been surpassed in population by Los Angeles.

East Indian spices, wiggly octopuses, silk saris, and live crabs. You'll smell tortillas baking and hear people speaking the languages of their native countries.

The CTA (Chicago Transit Authority) provides an efficient, cheap way to get around. Children under 7 (except large school groups) ride the buses, subways, and elevated lines for free. If you're between 7 and 11, public transportation fares are reduced (generally under $1.00). In warm weather, walking, riding bikes, roller skating, and even skateboarding are great ways to get around.

If you plan to visit the Windy City in winter, remember it really is windy! And cold! But if you bundle up, this great city, which sits by Lake Michigan and is straddled by the Chicago River (both its branches), is a winter wonderland of fun. Whatever the weather, Chicago can be your kind of town.

So, if you're ready for Chicago-style hot dogs, views from the top of the world, baseball, basketball, pork bellies, pyramids, parks, Picasso, mummies, sea mammals, submarines, space shuttles, zoo animals, the stars and the heavens above, jazz, blues, theater, symphonies, sculpture, skiing, skating, kite flying, souvenir buying, gangsters, and just about anything else you can think of, grab your copy of *Kidding Around Chicago* and get ready for one of the windiest cities of all, a city that's second to none, Frank Sinatra's "kind of town" and soon to be yours, too—Chicago!

When in the Windy City, remember that **Lake Michigan is always east**. The city follows a simple grid system with **Madison and State streets** at the baseline. The street numbers get higher the farther away in any direction you travel from Madison and State. The northern and southern parts of the city are divided by **Madison**. **State Street** separates eastern streets from western streets. You can't get lost in Chicago if you're traveling west or north. Every multiple of 800 represents a mile. So, for example, if you are at 800 N. Michigan, you are one mile north of the baseline.

2. Windy City Time Line

1600—Before this date, Chicago was inhabited by the Illinois, Miami, Wea, and Potawatomi Indians.

1673—Pere Jacques Marquette and Louis Joliet explore Chicago.

1779—Jean Baptiste Point Du Sable, Chicago's first permanent resident, builds his home near the banks of the Chicago River.

1804—Fort Dearborn is built to protect white settlers from Native Americans who are struggling to regain the area.

1806—By this time, Chicago is recognized as an important crossroads.

1812—Fort Dearborn is abandoned by the military. There is much fighting between whites and Native Americans.

1816—Fur trappers and traders and military personnel return to Fort Dearborn.

1832—Black Hawk, Chief of the Sac and Fox Indians, is defeated and forced to sign a treaty stating he will remain west of the Chicago River.

1833—Chicago has 300 residents and is officially incorporated.

1834—The first professional paid entertainment includes an exhibition of ventriloquism and fire eating. Admission: 25 cents.

1840—The Chicago Anti-Slavery Society holds its first public meeting.

1857—There are now 4,000 miles of railroad tracks connecting Chicago with other major U.S. cities.

1860—Abraham Lincoln, native of Illinois, is elected president of the United States.

1865—The Chicago Stockyards are opened.

1871—Mrs. O'Leary's cow kicks over a lantern, causing a fire that burns the entire town. Ninety thousand people are left homeless.

1870s—Famous architects begin to rebuild Chicago.

1894—Black and white railway workers strike to protest low wages.

1900—Chicago Sanitary and Ship Canal is completed to permanently and efficiently reverse the flow of the Chicago River.

1919—Gangster Al Capone, responsible for the 1929 St. Valentine's Day Massacre, comes to town.

1934—Gangster John Dillinger is killed at the Biograph movie theater by FBI agents.

1942—Scientists at the University of Chicago split the atom in a secret laboratory underneath the stands at Stagg Field.

1955—Richard J. Daley, one of the most famous mayors in U.S. history, is elected.

1968—The Democratic National Convention is held in Chicago and thousands of people protesting against the unpopular Vietnam War are beaten by police and National Guardsmen.

1975—Construction is completed on Sears Tower, the world's tallest skyscraper.

1983—Chicago's first black mayor, Harold Washington, is elected.

1985—State of Illinois Center Building opens.

1991—Chicago White Sox Comiskey Park reopens.

1992—Nike Town named biggest tourist attraction in Chicago.

3. River, Bird's-eye, Lakefront, and Elevated Views

Chicago, like all big cities, can be dangerous. Always travel with an adult, and if you get lost, stop a policeman or call 911 and someone will help you.

The best way to find your bearings in the Windy City is to view it from several angles—from the great **Chicago River** and **Lake Michigan**, from along miles of beachfront at Chicago's eastern edge, from a thousand feet above the city in the observation deck of **Sears Tower**, and from the hair-raising roller coaster, **Ravenswood Elevated Subway Line**.

If you cross the river at Michigan Avenue and walk toward downtown, you will cross the **Michigan Avenue Bridge**, one of Chicago's 50 or so drawbridges. At any moment the bridge might be raised to give passage to a ship on its way upriver. (Don't worry about walking over bridges. Pedestrian and motor traffic is always cleared before bridges go up.)

The river used to flow into Lake Michigan until 1836, when Chicagoans built a temporary canal (the **Illinois-Michigan Canal**) that, through the force of gravity, caused the sluggish Chicago River to reverse its course. In 1900, the **Sanitary and Ship Canal** was built. The new permanent canal kept the water flowing from the lake into the river. This was done to keep the city's waste from polluting the lake, Chicago's main source of drinking water. The Windy City's drinking water is now considered the cleanest of any urban area.

Chicagoans use the lake to play in as well as to drink from. To get a real feel of the city from the lake and the river, pack a p.b. & j. and hop on a **Wendella Sightseeing Boat** (Wendella's offices are in the Wrigley Building). Check out the skyline as the boat winds up and down the river and onto Lake Michigan.

Or cruise over to the south side of Michigan Avenue at the **Mercury Dock** and steal your way onto a **Wacky Pirate Cruise**. The buccaneers on

The Sears Tower looks down on the heart of Chicago

Photo courtesy of Peter J. Schultz / City of Chicago

11

board will give you a kazoo, tell you haunting tales of high seas, and spin a yarn or two about pirates who sailed Lake Michigan.

When you are back on dry land again, walk along Wacker Drive and look north across the bridge. Now you have a great view of the **Wrigley Building**, corporate headquarters of Wrigley chewing gum. Slightly east of the Wrigley Building and west of the **Equitable Building** is where some historians believe Chicago's first recorded resident, Jean Baptiste Point Du Sable, built his home sometime around 1779. Du Sable, of African and French descent, made his home on the banks of the Chicago River with his Native American wife.

As you walk west along the river, you will come to the original site of **Fort Dearborn** on N. Michigan and Wacker, built by white men to protect new settlers and this major crossroads of commerce from the area's original settlers, the Potawatomi Indians.

But the fort didn't help them for long. On August 15, 1812, the Potawatomi attacked Fort Dearborn. Many were killed, and the fort commander's wife was captured. She was bought back for the price of one mule and ten bottles of whiskey. The Potawatomi eventually lost all hold on the area, and, as you can see, the brass plaques in the sidewalk are the only reminders of the fort and those earlier days.

Farther west at **Wolf Point**, right across the **Franklin-Orleans Bridge**, is where the branches of the Chicago River meet. While there are no historic markers, and no one is quite sure where the name Wolf Point comes from, there are many stories floating around the city that this was the site of a trading post in 1778 and later the site of a rough-and-tumble tavern called the Rat Castle. Seeing the sky lined with towering

The folks at Wrigley say Americans chew just under 300 sticks of gum per person, each year.

skyscrapers, it's hard to imagine Chicago's wild frontier times.

The tallest building of all in Chicago is the 1,454-foot (1,707 feet if you include the two white antennas on top of the building) **Sears Tower** at N. Wacker and Adams.

It's not your imagination, that is the wind you hear howling as you step into the Sears Tower elevators that soar 1,353 feet in 55 seconds, carrying you up to the 103rd-floor **Skydeck Observatory**. You won't be able to feel it, but the 110-story building actually sways during strong winds. Don't worry, engineers built it that way to withstand the stormiest weather. So unless you feel uneasy about towering over the rest of the world, take a trip to the top and get a bird's-eye view of Chicago.

As you peer out of the bronze tinted windows, you can see the John Hancock Center to the north, the Adler Planetarium and the expanse of Lake Michigan to the east, and Comiskey Park, home of the Chicago White Sox to the south. As you look west, you will see how quickly the tall cityscape gives way to smaller neighborhood buildings.

Unless you're interested in miles of mist, don't waste time or money going up to the Observatory when there is zero visibility. (Zero visibility means you can't see a thing.)

Hop into your hightops and walk, ride bikes, roller skate, or skateboard along part of Chicago's 29 miles of beachfront. You can get bike trail maps from Chicago's Bureau of Traffic Engineering and Operations on N. Clark Street. Most bicycle rental shops in the city do not specifically rent kids' bikes, but you may find a bike that is right for you at **Bicycles Chicago Rental** on W. Randolph. In warm weather, you can rent bikes in Lincoln Park.

*Kids at **Francis Parker School** discovered Chicagoans will produce over 2.5 million tons of garbage by 1994. The city's landfills will be full and the garbage will have no place to go. Even while traveling, you can recycle.*

13

The city began to develop the lakefront as a recreational area in the 1930s. Prior to this, the area consisted of miles of mucky muddy marshland. An Illinois state law declares the lakefront shall remain forever "open, clear, and free" so everyone can enjoy it.

You can find roller skates at **United Skates of America** on N. Clark and cruise the lakefront beaches. These sandy shores aren't like California beaches, but sand combined with long stretches of concrete walkways and rusted piers are Chicago's version of beaches, and Chicagoans are proud of them.

There are many underground passageways that will allow you to avoid having to cross traffic-laden Lake Shore Drive. These passageways take you right out to the water's edge. During summer months, don't forget to bring your fishing pole out to the beach. Lake Michigan is full of perch and coho salmon.

Another way to be on the edge of the city is to catch the Ravenswood "EL" or ("L") subway line

from the **Quincy/Wells/Loop L station**. Take this train around the loop to a neighborhood called **Albany Park**, where you can get out, wander around a bit, and have a bite of curried chicken with coconut milk at the **Thai Little Home Cafe** on Kedzie Avenue. But if this roller coaster "L" of a ride has you holding onto your hat and your stomach, you may want to wait until you get back to the Quincy/Wells station to have a slice of pizza at **Giordano's** on Wabash and Jackson.

As the train heads back into the city, you will get a great view of some of Chicago's many ethnic neighborhoods as well as a dramatic view of the city's skyline from the northwest.

Now you're ready to do some more exploring, touring, eating, shopping, and even some space shuttle riding.

The renovated Quincy/Wells/Loop L station used to be heated by a potbelly stove. Before you step onto the train, look up at the ceilings. The molded tin looks the way it did in 1897.

4. Succulents, Simians, and Sea Lions (Lincoln Park/Depaul)

Lincoln Park, on Chicago's north side, is the city's largest park. Situated on 12,000 acres, it has 12 beaches, several museums, and a zoo with over 2,000 birds, mammals, and reptiles. It was used as a cemetery from 1810 to 1842. When the city decided to make it a park, thousands of bodies were moved to the city's other cemeteries. There may still be people buried there. As recently as the early 1980s, workmen widening the road discovered skeletons from several unmarked graves.

You won't find human skeletons in the **Chicago Historical Society**, but you can get a hands-on feel for some of Chicago's well-preserved historical events.

Touch beaver, badger, or muskrat skins, like ones used by the Potawatomi and fur traders as a means of barter. How many beaver skins would you pay to buy a cast iron skillet or a wool blanket?

In the **Pioneer Life Gallery**, you can see very authentic-looking pioneer women as they dip candles and weave on a loom built in the early 1800s.

Produce your own old-time radio show in the **Hands-on History Exhibit** using blocks of wood to create the sound of a gunshot or sheets of metal to make the sound of thunder, and then climb aboard the engine of the **Pioneer**, the first train to come through the city of Chicago in 1848.

Save a bird: make a falcon silhouette for your window to protect small birds from flying into the glass. Lincoln Park Zoo Review *reminds you: don't wear belts, shoes, or coats made from endangered species.*

As you leave the museum and head north, you will see a big red barn. That's right, it's a farm right in the middle of the city, known as the **Farm-in-the-Zoo**. The farm has several different barns with horses, cows, pigs, and chickens. In the Dairy Barn, you'll see how the butter you eat gets from cow to kitchen table. To watch the farm animals being fed, visit the barns around 9:00 a.m. or at about 3:00 p.m.

After watching the animals eat their dinners, you might be pretty hungry yourself, so head to the **Cafe Brauer**, where hamburgers and hot dogs are served year-round. If you're not starving, wait and grab a Chicago-style hot dog at **Gold Coast Dogs** on the corner of N. Clark and W. Dickens.

If you still need to work up an appetite, you can rent pedal boats and pedal your way around **South Pond** or take a 30-minute walk around the pond's perimeter. You might see some wood ducks, mallards, and a fish or two.

But head on to the Sea Lion Pool at the **Lincoln Park Zoo** to see some real swimming. Even in the dead of winter, the seals and sea lions seem to be sunning themselves as if they were vacationing at a seaside resort.

You'll go ape at the Great Ape House, which houses one of the largest collections of apes in captivity in the entire world. It's downright eerie to watch gorillas with names like Debbie and Frank as they watch you watching them. Don't stare too much or they might start pounding on

Doing some shopping at the Chicago Historical Society

Photo courtesy of Chicago Historical Society

Koundu, one of Lincoln Park Zoo's male lowland gorillas, watches over his "kingdom" in the backyard of the Great Ape House.

the glass. Gorillas, like all animals, need peace and quiet. So, please, be respectful when visiting the zoo.

To get a feel for some feline feelings, visit the endangered cats like snow leopards, cheetahs, and Siberian tigers at the new Kovler Lion House.

At last count, more than 200 mammals, reptiles, and birds were born or hatched at the zoo. Many of these animals are considered to be threatened, endangered, or critically endangered species. To learn how Lincoln Park Zoo is working to help save the world's animals, become a member of the zoo and read the ***Zoo Review***, which lists current and upcoming workshops and events for children at the **Crown-Field Center** and at the Children's Zoo.

At the **Lincoln Park Children's Zoo** (considered the first children's zoo in the country to be

open year-round), you can see baby animals like Tabibu, a gorilla born in May 1992. She'll remind you of your kid sister as she sucks her thumb and stumbles around in her diapers. If you are careful and gentle, you might get a chance to pet goats and guinea pigs and maybe even an armadillo. It all depends on how the animals are feeling. Zoo officials explain that animals get stressed out just like people do and sometimes need to be left alone.

If *you're* stressed out and need to get away from the crowds that frequent the zoo (the world's busiest), take a break and walk to the **Lincoln Park Conservatory** and stroll through a jungle of exotic plants. This gigantic greenhouse features a 50-foot rubber tree from Africa and all kinds of weird exotic tropical plants from India, Brazil, and China.

At the recently reopened **McCormick Bird House**, see Toco toucans, Blyth's hornbills, and the rare and endangered Bali myna.

Meet a friendly python at the Chicago Academy of Sciences.

Photo courtesy of Debra Naevel/Chicago Academy of Sciences

Seals and sea lions are different. Sea lions have small external ears. Seals have small ear openings. Sea lions get around more easily. They use front flippers to negotiate, while seals use their hind flippers. Sea lions make a lot more noise than seals. Which are you more likely to see climbing on the rocks at the zoo? Seals or sea lions?

The birds at the **Chicago Academy of Sciences** can't fly; as a matter of fact, most of the animals here don't move at all because they're stuffed! The Academy, just west of Cafe Brauer and across Stockton Drive, has a stuffed moose, bears, birds, wolves, and models of prehistoric fish. In the recently renovated North Gallery, see special temporary exhibits like "Why Waste a Good Planet?" This hands-on exhibit re-creates a typical American home and asks you what you would do to conserve energy.

Do you have a deep dark desire to touch creepy crawly creatures? Learn how to handle snakes and bugs or how to go spelunking through the Academy's bat caves. You can even take an overnight excursion and learn how to make a traditional Native American medicine bag and use a mono and a matate. Academy of Sciences exhibits and workshops change month to month, so call ahead to find out current schedules to avoid disappointment.

You won't be disappointed by the Academy's Gift Shop, which has a great assortment of sparkling bismuth crystals, models of fossils and dinosaurs, chemistry sets, and even a disappearing ink kit.

If you've had your fill of museum activities, visit one of Lincoln Park's twelve beaches. The best beaches for kids in this area are right north or south of Diversey Street. If you are knee deep in snow, try some cross-country skiing. To find out about cross-country ski trails, the best hills for sledding, and the cool places to ice skate, call the **Chicago Parks District** on Lincoln Park West.

Just west and a bit north of Lincoln Park in the Lincoln Park/Depaul area are nifty shops like **Wax Trax**, a local record shop hangout for kids, the **Children's Bookstore**, which has a small platform and stage for a story-telling hour and features the biggest selection of children's books in Chicago, and **Women and Children First**, another young reader's favorite—all on N. Lincoln.

Wanna be rowdy? Have a char-dog, boogie to the jukebox, and play a few rounds of Pop-a-Shot Basketball at **Michael's** on N. Clark, or go to **R. J. Grunts** just a few blocks away on N. Lincoln, where you can grab a bowl of chili and boogaloo to '60s Motown. For a look at some great films from every era, take a seat at **Facets Multimedia**, an alternative movie house on Fullerton, and see old Charlie Chaplin films and children's classics like *Heidi* and *National Velvet*.

There are some gruesome gangster landmarks in this area you won't want to miss, including the site of the 1929 **St. Valentine's Day Massacre** (2122 N. Clark St.), where seven men were gunned down. Most of the victims, members of George "Bugs" Moran's gang, were shot by men masquerading as police officers. When Moran heard the news that his men were dead, he said, "Only Capone kills like that," referring to rival gangster Al Capone.

*Gangster Machine Gun Jake McGurn, hit man at the St. Valentine's Day Massacre, met **his** end while bowling at 805 N. Milwaukee (now a store). His killers left him with the following valentine: "You've lost your job, you've lost your dough, Your jewels and cars and handsome houses! Things could be worse, you know— At least you haven't lost your trousas!"*

21

Another famous spot is the **Biograph Theater** on N. Lincoln Avenue, where bank robber John Dillinger was ambushed by federal authorities on July 22, 1934, at 10:40 p.m. after watching a movie called *Manhattan Melodrama*. There are dents in a telephone pole near the theater. People claim these are from the bullets fired by federal agents who waited for Dillinger. They were tipped off by the criminal's girlfriend, the mysterious Lady in Red. Dillinger was shot dead on the spot.

If you're a Dead Head, you'll appreciate golfing at **Par Excellence**, an indoor miniature golf range at 1800 Clybourn Mall. Designed by a local Chicago artist, the 18th hole looks like a graveyard filled with hundreds of tiny skeletons. In the same mall, be sure to check out the spanking brand new branch of **Barbara's Bookstore** packed with bundles of books for kids.

Not far from there lies **Oz Park**, between Lincoln, Halsted, and Armitage streets. This small park is frequented by big and little kids alike. There are wooden ships, bridges, and castles to explore. The park was named for the famous story, "The Wizard of Oz," created by Chicagoans Frank Baum and W. D. Denslow. This kooky collaboration led to the invention of Dorothy, Toto, the Tin Man, the Cowardly Lion, the Scarecrow, and all those little Munchkins!

5. Cows and Rock 'n Roll (Near North, North Pier, River North)

T here are several exciting neighborhoods south of Lincoln Park and north of the Chicago River. These areas are bounded by Lake Michigan on the east and the north branch of the Chicago River on the west.

You'll hear people refer to one of Chicago's posh sections as **Magnificent Mile, Boul Mich** (short for Boulevard Michigan), or **Miracle Mile**. All the different names mean the same thing— lots of expensive stores.

Even if you don't have money to burn, you'll want to step inside **Water Tower Place** to ride in the glass elevator or cruise on escalators that can transport up to 18,000 people an hour from shop to shop. The mall has a Gap Kids and a McDonald's. F.A.O. Schwarz (for even more kid stuff, a larger F.A.O. Schwarz will open across the street) carries everything from giant stuffed bears to Teenage Mutant Ninja Turtles. ROCS will knock your socks off with its nifty earrings and doodads to delight. At Arcadia, pick up a wild T-shirt or a wacky neon clock that laughs.

After you've had your fill of the frivolous, walk across to the Water Tower whence the shopping area takes its name.

When the smoke settled after the Great Chicago Fire, started on the night of October 8, 1871, two of the few buildings to survive the

*A branch of Barbara's Bookstore, which has one of the greatest selections of kids' books in Chicago, is in an area called **Old Town**, a bit north and west of the Boul Mich. North and east of Boul Mich buy a Windy City T-shirt and eat an Elvis Hound Dog at Boogie's Diner Retail in the **Near North** area. Above Near North and below Lincoln Park lies a wealthy residential area known as the **Gold Coast**.*

catastrophe were the **Water Tower Pumping Station** and the **Water Tower**, castlelike buildings constructed of limestone. No one is really sure how the fire began, but the most popular story is that Mrs. O'Leary's cow kicked over a lantern, setting the O'Leary barn ablaze. The flames spread out of control, and most of the city's wooden structures burned to the ground. Three hundred people were killed, and 90,000 were left homeless.

Pizza experts claim that Americans eat 75 acres of pizza a day.

Today the Pumping Station, which is still in operation, houses a tourist attraction called **Here's Chicago**, where you can learn about the station's history. (During hot summer days, the station is capable of pumping 260 million gallons of water throughout the city of Chicago.) Here you'll also see a life-size model of **Mrs. O'Leary's cow**, a reenactment of the St. Valentine's Day Massacre, and lifelike models of detective Elliot Ness and gangster Al Capone. At the end of the tour, see a film called *City of Dreams*. The film, shot from a helicopter, lets you get a feel for Chicago from on high.

After you leave Here's Chicago, get a sky-high view of the city by visiting the world's third tallest building, the **John Hancock Center** on N. Michigan. This building resembles a humongous insect with its towering antennas. On a clear day you can see four states (Indiana, Illinois, Michigan, and Wisconsin).

The **Terra Museum of American Art** on N. Michigan has paintings by Andrew Wyeth. After you've looked at his farm scenes, take a ride in the museum's huge room-size elevator used to carry large works of art upstairs.

If you're lucky when you visit the **Museum of Contemporary Art** on E. Ontario, you might get to see some pretty wild performance artists like Vito Acconci, who used his body to create living sculpture, or you might get to see the entire building wrapped like an enormous birthday present by the artist, Christo.

Museum hopping can work up an appetite, so you may want to mosey over to **Pizzeria Uno** (or **Pizzeria Due** up the block), home of the original deep dish Chicago pizza, on E. Ohio Street, or have a slice at **Gino's** on E. Superior, then hop on a Grand Avenue bus and head toward the newly renovated **North Pier**. Here you'll find a mall packed with video arcades, stores, and two great museums.

Whatever you do, give yourself plenty of time to build, touch, bubble, creep, crawl, and create your way through the fabulous, just for kids **Chicago Children's Museum**. As you enter the museum you will see the Recycle Arts Center. For $3.50, pick up a paper bag and fill it full of doorknobs, wooden blocks, pieces of cardboard, tiny bits of carpeting, little plastic doo-hickeys that look like tiny spaceships, and tons of other recycled industrial junk and create something.

You can make your own Latin American folk dolls, robots, purses, money pouches, pillows— anything you can think of. From there, walk through the museum's Amazing Chicago and see a replica of the city with kid-sized buildings. It's a great way to get a sense of Chicago's architecture. Next, negotiate through City Hospital's wheelchair obstacle course. Step inside a model of an ambulance, take a look at real x-rays, and don't miss the Velcro heart, liver, and lungs! At the Stinking Truth about Garbage, grab your hard hat, your flashlight, and your nose (not really) as you tromp through a mock landfill. Exhibits change periodically, so check to avoid disappointment. At the Art and Science of

Bubbles Exhibit, surround yourself in huge people-sized bubbles, and at Magic and Masquerades, create West African masks, beaded jewelry, and costumes. Recycle, discover, express yourself!

For a look at some ships, take a walk outside at North Pier. Here you can stroll, watch the boats on the lake, and get a great view of the city. In warm weather, you can walk out onto Grand Avenue and explore **Navy Pier**, built in 1916 for commercial shipping. In 1976, the city of Chicago renovated the 3,000-foot pier, making it available for a variety of uses including fairs and art exhibitions.

The nearby **City of Chicago Store** on E. Illinois Street is a good place to pick up Chicago posters, sweatshirts, books on the city, or a Lincoln Park Zoo belt buckle. Or how about a T-shirt with a picture of Chicago's L system and the words, "I had a 'L' of a time in Chicago."

River North, Chicago's arty neighborhood west of Dearborn Street and a bit east of the north branch of the Chicago River, is sometimes referred to as **Suhu** (which means the area near Superior and Huron streets). Most people think "New York" when they think "modern art," but Chicago's River North is a large, vital artist community with over 50 galleries. The exhibitions here aren't geared to kids, but if the big people you are traveling with are gallery hopping, you will find plenty to see and do in the general area.

A bit out of the way but not too far from the River North area on W. Chicago is the **_Chicago Tribune_ Freedom Center**, the plant where the _Tribune_ is printed. Kids over the age of ten can take a tour and see old _Trib_ headlines from the first moon landing and the day Abraham Lincoln was elected president.

If you need a rest from historical sights and museums, stop for a munchies break and a boisterous trip down rock-and-roll memory lane at **Ed Debevik's** eatery extraordinaire on N. Wells Street. The signs read "Ed's Chili Dog—The Cadillac of Chili Dogs," and waitresses are rocking to '50s tunes in their bobby socks. From there, bop on over to W. Ontario Street, where kids can, and do, hang out at the **Hard Rock Cafe** until evening hours. Here you can see Indiana Jones's leather jacket and Michael Jackson's platinum records, not to mention half of a Cadillac sticking out of the wall. Take one more step down memory lane and check out the **Rock 'n' Roll McDonald's** on N. Clark. The world's busiest, this home of the golden arches houses life-size statues of the Beatles and is open 24 hours a day. So grab a burger, sip your shake next to the 1959 Corvette parked in the window, and cool out!

6. The Loop: Pork Bellies, Cattle, and Calder (Downtown)

he "**Loop**" technically refers to the area within the loop made by elevated tracks that encircle Chicago's downtown area. The Loop also refers to the general area between Lake Michigan on the east, the Chicago River on the west and north, and Congress Parkway (some say even as far as Roosevelt Road) on the south.

You may need a couple of days to see everything in the Loop area. You'll probably want to spend at least one day exploring Chicago's inner Loop and another day downtown investigating more museums, stores, and buildings. However you decide to break it up, there are tons of great places you won't want to miss.

At the center of the Loop is the hustling, bustling financial hub of the midwestern United States. This area is also the center of government offices, some Chicago landmark buildings, and the city's great outdoor sculpture.

LaSalle Street became the city's financial center in 1865 with the building of the Board of Trade. Destroyed and rebuilt after the great Chicago Fire, the area surrounding the Board quickly grew to be a hotbed for commerce and the focus of modern architecture.

The Art Deco **Chicago Board of Trade Building** stands at the end of LaSalle, hovering above the rest of Chicago's financial district. Perched on

By 1837, the year Chicago officially became incorporated, there were 4,000 people living in the city, most of them in and around the area that is now known as the Loop. The Chicago metro area now has about 7 million people, many of whom work in the downtown area.

If you are a trader, you'll never see a real pork belly (the stuff that ham and bacon are made of) or a soybean. Traders speculate, or guess, what they think the price of a certain product will be in the future.

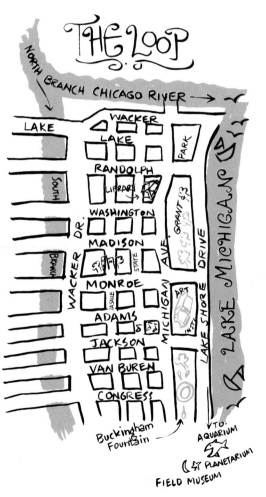

the very top of the building is a faceless statue of **Ceres**, the Greek goddess of grain. She stands like a guardian angel over Chicago's largest and oldest futures exchange. At the **Visitor's Gallery** on the fifth floor, see how futures on things like corn, soybeans, and wheat are traded. The trading pit is the same area traders worked in almost 100 years ago. Before the use of computers, prices were written on a blackboard.

Across the street is the **Chicago Board Options Exchange**. Here you can also see what you saw at the board of trade—the "open outcry system." Translation: guys and girls dressed in funny bright-colored jackets standing around screaming and waving their arms, making and losing money.

From here, you can head up to the **Chicago Mercantile Exchange** on S. Wacker, but first take a look at the nautilus-shaped indoor fire escape at the **Rookery** on S. LaSalle Street, with its remodeled lobby by "Chicago school" architect, Frank Lloyd Wright. A plaque states this is Chicago's oldest skyscraper.

At the Merc, they are trading futures on live cattle, live hogs, pork bellies, and some financial products. The **Visitor's Gallery** on the fourth floor features an interactive video for kids explaining futures trading.

Whether you plan on stashing your cash under your pillow or investing in some soybeans, these financial centers will give you a good look at capitalism at work.

Money makes the world go around. So does politics. At the **Chicago City Hall-Cook County Building**, on Clark between Randolph and Washington, you may get to see some more shouting and arm waving if you happen by during one of Chicago's famous City Council meetings.

While Chicago may be known for LaSalle Street deals and heated political arguments in City Hall, it is also famous for its architecture. A great way to get an overview of Chicago's architectural history is to stop in at the **Chicago Architecture Foundation** on S. Dearborn. You can sign up for a tour of architectural sights designed especially for kids. This short walking tour traces the development of the skyscraper. You'll see buildings designed by Frank Lloyd Wright, Louis Sullivan, and Ludwig Mies van der Rohe, some of the most famous architects the world has ever known.

World-famous artists have also left their mark in Chicago in the form of magnificent outdoor sculpture, all within a few blocks of one another. Here are a few of them.

The Jean Dubuffet sculpture, *Monument with Standing Beast*, looks like a goofy gargoyle as it guards the entrance to the **State of Illinois Center** on Randolph Street. You can climb around on this beast and then walk inside the Star Wars-like spaceship of a building.

No Luke Skywalkers, Darth Vaders, or Han Solos in this spaceship, just somber-looking business types in blue suits. But you'll feel like you're being beamed up to the bridge when you ride the clear glass elevator all the way to the top of the building.

Just south of the Illinois Center at the **Daley Center**, named for the late Chicago Mayor Richard J. Daley, stands the famous rusty Picasso sculpture. It has no name other than "The Picasso." Some people say it's the head of a woman. Some say it's a cow. Still others insist it's an Afghan hound. What do you think? The plaza area around the Daley Center is a popular warm weather hangout for young skateboarders from all parts of the city. In winter, bring your ice

The 24,600 glass panels in the State of Illinois Center conducted so much heat during the building's first years that people were forced to wear tropical clothes in summer to keep cool.

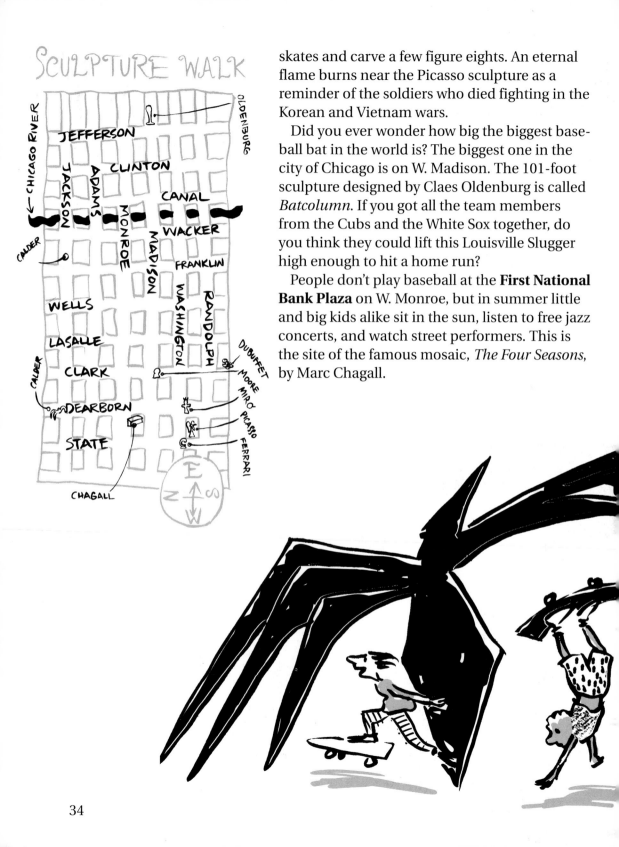

SCULPTURE WALK

Map labels:
OLDENBURG
CHICAGO RIVER
JEFFERSON
JACKSON
ADAMS
CLINTON
CANAL
MONROE
WACKER
MADISON
FRANKLIN
WASHINGTON
RANDOLPH
WELLS
LASALLE
CALDER
CLARK
DUBUFFET
MOORE
MIRÓ
PICASSO
FERRARI
DEARBORN
STATE
CHAGALL
CALDER

E N S W

skates and carve a few figure eights. An eternal flame burns near the Picasso sculpture as a reminder of the soldiers who died fighting in the Korean and Vietnam wars.

Did you ever wonder how big the biggest base-ball bat in the world is? The biggest one in the city of Chicago is on W. Madison. The 101-foot sculpture designed by Claes Oldenburg is called *Batcolumn*. If you got all the team members from the Cubs and the White Sox together, do you think they could lift this Louisville Slugger high enough to hit a home run?

People don't play baseball at the **First National Bank Plaza** on W. Monroe, but in summer little and big kids alike sit in the sun, listen to free jazz concerts, and watch street performers. This is the site of the famous mosaic, *The Four Seasons*, by Marc Chagall.

South of the Xerox building on S. Dearborn stands *Flamingo* by the artist Alexander Calder, inventor of the "mobile." This sculpture, a "stabile," may not look like a bird to you. What would you call it?

As you can see, within a few blocks you can get a good look at some of the world's most famous modern art, and you don't even have to step inside a museum.

The famous Picasso sculpture in the Daley Center Plaza in Chicago.

Photo courtesy of Chicago Office of Tourism

*The Alexander Calder sculpture, **Universe**, in the entrance of the Sears Tower is the artist's largest moving mobile-like mural.*

7. More Loop

Near Randolph and Wells is where, in 1834, the Chippewa, Ottawa, and Potawatomi Indians were paid for the remaining portions of their land and forced to leave the Chicago area.

Another historic spot is at 100 W. Monroe Street, where there is a cow path that was reserved for farmer Willard Jones's cow. A 1938 city ordinance states cows are to be allowed to walk through the Loop between 7:00 a.m. and 7:00 p.m. There aren't many cows grazing through Chicago these days, but if you plan to bring a bovine buddy with you when you visit, you'll know where to take it.

In 1899, architect Louis Sullivan designed the Schlesinger and Mayer store, which is now called the **Carson Pirie Scott and Company Building** on S. State Street. Make sure to take a look at the rounded windows and delicately detailed ironwork above the entrance to the building. This is a prize example of what's known as the "Chicago school of architecture" at its most ornamental stage.

Another famous department store is **Marshall Field's** on N. State Street, which sells "famous" Frango Mints, the best chocolate in the world. For generations, people have shopped here and used the huge outdoor clock as a meeting place. But when you look, you'll see two clocks. In

Chicago, if someone says, "I'll meet you under the Marshall Field's clock," it means the one near Randolph, not the one near Washington. Be sure to go inside to the Crystal Palace, an old-fashioned ice cream parlor, and have a squiggly sundae with gummy spiders, worms, and insects. If you're bugged by bugs, you can also order a plain scoop.

In the old days, a scoop or two might have been what you'd have after an afternoon of comedy at the old **Chicago Theater** on N. State, where the Marx Brothers, Bob Hope, and Jerry Lewis all performed. The theater, built in 1921, was almost demolished in 1982, but Chicagoans put up a fuss. It was restored, and now you may be able to catch an ice show, a magic show, or a musical extravaganza.

For comic relief, head to **Comic Relief** on E. Madison, a small friendly store with new and used comic books. Some rare comics sell for up to $30,000. This store doesn't carry anything that pricey. But they do have a big selection of new and used Batman and Spiderman comics and lots of X-Men titles.

You can take your comic books and read them over at the **Harold Washington Library Center** on S. State. The library offers all kinds of special programs including puppet shows, mimes, jugglers, and musicians. There have even been special workshops on pet care and proper manners!

Proper manners are essential when attending a Chicago Symphony Orchestra concert at **Orchestra Hall** on S. Michigan; no fidgeting, whispering, or running around here.

But if you don't feel like behaving yourself, go make some noise in Grant Park. In summer, fly a kite, play baseball, and visit Buckingham Fountain, where you can see a nighttime light show or listen to music during the world-

*Whether you hear a concert in the park, see a puppet show at **Hystopolis Puppet Theater,** kick up your heels and sing along with a musical production at **ETA Creative Arts Foundation**, or visit **Second City's Children's Theater**, you'll want to check for dates and locations of specific performances. Pick up a copy of the* Chicago Reader, *a free weekly paper,* Chicago Magazine, *or the* Sunday Chicago Tribune *and check for children's listings.*

Two kids celebrate getting their first library card at the Woodson Branch Library.

Photo courtesy of Gary Degnan/ Chicago Office of Tourism

The largest hand-launched kite ever flown in Grant Park was 83 feet long. Chicago is a great place to fly kites. It really is the Windy City.

famous Gospel, Blues, and Jazz Fests. During July, you won't want to miss Taste of Chicago, the city's biggest food festival offering thousands of sumptuous samplings. The James C. Petrillo Music Shell hosts the Grant Park Concert Series.

Whether you're listening to a concert, batting a ball, or passing the pigskin, remember to say hello to Abraham Lincoln. A statue of the Illinois-born president stands in between Buckingham Fountain and the **Art Institute** on S. Michigan, a museum packed with statues and Seurat's famous *A Sunday Afternoon on the Island of La Grande Jatte*, a huge painting made up entirely of dots.

But you don't have to tromp through the entire museum to see great artwork. The Art Institute designed a kid-size museum called the Kraft General Foods Education Center featuring "Art Inside Out," an interactive art gallery. You can paint there, or bring a sack lunch to the picnic room and take a break. You might get to see someone like Lamanidi Fakeye, a fifth-generation Yoruba wood carver from Nigeria, as he demonstrates African wood carving techniques.

The Kraft Center also features special programs throughout the year. You can learn how to make Japanese fans or help paint huge murals.

In the Family Room, find out how to be a regular Sherlock Holmes by playing "I Spy," a game that will have you running all over the museum discovering the answers to mysterious clues.

Chicago-style blues music was born in the 1930s when many musicians from the South came to the Windy City and began adding new guitar techniques to traditional blues music. Chicago Blues had its heyday in the 1950s. Some Chicago Blues greats: Muddy Waters, James Cotton, and Buddy Guy.

And, of course, on your way in or out, don't forget to say hello to two of Chicago's most beloved animals, the bronze lions that guard the entrance to the Art Institute. In 1986, the Chicago Bears won the Super Bowl. After the game fans adorned the famous felines with football helmets.

The **Maurice Spertus Museum of Judaica**, just south of the Art Institute on S. Michigan, has a permanent, hands-on exhibit of Near Eastern archaeology for kids called the Artifact Center.

Two blocks north of the Art Institute, you'll find the **Museum of Broadcast Communications** at N. Michigan and Washington, where you and a partner can have 15 minutes of fame in front of the camera reading the teleprompter, reporting the news, and giving sports scores as anchors of your own news show. You can spend hours reviewing tapes of the TV shows your parents used to watch, like "Dobie Gillis," "Lost in Space," and "The Flintstones."

8. Mollies, Mummies, and Moon Rocks (South of the Loop)

It's easy to forget, but mummies are people too. An often asked question is, "What are mummies made of?" Mummies are dead people or animals that have been preserved.

hicago is famous for its **Field Museum of Natural History** on S. Lake Shore Drive which owns about 19,000,000 bones, stones, and all kinds of artifacts. Originally opened in 1894, it has over nine acres of exhibits to see, touch, hear, feel, and investigate.

But as one Chicago kid warns, "The Field Museum is very, very big, very hot, and you can get very tired in there!" It's true. It is big and hot, and you can get tired in there, but for goodness sake, don't let that stop you. An important piece of advice for you and any adults you may be kidding around with: Don't try to see or do too much. A good idea is to visit this museum and focus on one or two sections. When you get tired, go outside and play frisbee.

Some Chicago kid favorites at the Field Museum are the Sizes Exhibit, the Skeleton and Reptile Hall, Into the Wild: Animal Trails and Tales, the Traveling Pacific Exhibit, and the Inside Ancient Egypt Exhibit. At the Sizes Exhibit on the first floor, try on the biggest pair of blue jeans ever made. These giant-sized overalls are big enough for at least two whole regular-sized kids. There is a table and chair that will remind big kids of what it felt like to be three years old, and there is also the optical illusion room that will make you shrink and grow like magic!

WHAT'S A MUMMY'S FAVORITE MUSIC?

RAP!

Jr. scientists: Recheck facts. New discoveries are made all the time, and even experts make mistakes.

In the Skeleton and Reptile Hall on the first floor, there are backbones, leg bones, jawbones, and craniums. In Into the Wild, don't miss the 45-foot whale skeleton hanging from the ceiling. How many Jonahs do you think this whale could've swallowed?

At the south end of Stanley Field Hall on the first floor sits a 6H-foot-long, 100-million-year-old thigh bone of a brachiosaurus. This dynamo of a dinosaur weighed in at more than 85.63 tons. He apparently had a tiny mouth and lots of bad teeth.

To see what peoples of the Pacific ate, walk through a turn-of-the-century New Guinea village at one of the museum's newest features, the Traveling the Pacific Exhibit on the second floor. You can sit in the Spirit Canoe and test your navigational skills with the Seafaring Survival computer game. With only the stars, meager provisions, and crew, will you be able to master the high seas?

You won't need a caravan of camels to climb 35 feet down into the reconstructed 4,000-year-old tomb of Unis-ankh, the son of an ancient pharaoh. The Inside Ancient Egypt Exhibit has 23 real mummies. The mummy of Harwa, found in the Egyptian city of Karnak, looks pretty good for being almost 3,000 years old!

To avoid total exhaustion, make a pit stop at the **McDonald's** or the **Snack Bar**, both in the museum's basement, before you head over to the Shedd Aquarium.

You'll want to get to the **John G. Shedd Aquarium** before the sharks, sea turtles, and moray eels get their daily meals at 11:00 a.m., 2:00 p.m., and 3:00 p.m. A diver, equipped with a special microphone, can answer questions while diving into the 90,000-gallon tank to feed all of the 200 tropical fish. The sharks go crazy, the moray eels sometimes nibble at the diver's heels, and the sea turtles get downright snappy.

In April 1991, the world's largest indoor aquarium opened an oceanarium with 3-million-gallon habitats to house sea otters, beluga whales, Pacific white side dolphins, harbor seals, and penguins. There was quite a controversy over the opening of the oceanarium. Many people think it's cruel to keep large sea mammals in captivity. What do you think?

East of the aquarium sits the **Adler Planetarium**, where if you look west, you'll get a spectacular view of the Chicago skyline. Your exposure to the universe starts with a zippy multimedia show in the Universe Theater which includes several films and slides projected onto the ceiling and walls. From there, be launched toward the heavens in the Sky Theater where you will see how the stars and planets move across the sky.

After the show, travel to the space transporters and beam yourself up to Venus in the **Hall of Space Exploration.** Step into specially designed booths that show you the difference between your body weight on Earth and your weight on other planets in the solar system.

Don't miss the sharp space suit worn by U.S. astronauts and the 4-billion-year-old moon rock picked up by David Scott, one of the astronauts aboard the Apollo 15 mission.

In the gift shop, you can find space patches, gemstone rings, astronomy capsules, and a prism scope. If you're hungry, have some astronaut food or head out to **Burnham Park** for a picnic.

Meigs Field, across from Burnham Park, is a private airstrip, and from time to time daredevil flyers, the Blue Angels, leave their trail across the sky. Directly across from Meigs Field is **Soldier**

The Shedd Aquarium is the only place outside of the West Coast where you can see Alaskan sea otters that were saved after the 1989 Exxon Valdez oil spill.

Feeling pretty skinny? Wait 'til you get to Jupiter. If you weigh 96 pounds on Earth, you'd weigh 235 pounds on Jupiter.

Field, where the Chicago Bears put on a show of their own during football season.

Just southwest of Meigs, you may want to stop in at **McCormick Place**, the largest exhibition hall in America. There might be a boat show, a car show, or the National Gin Rummy Tournament.

North and west of McCormick Place in the **Prairie Avenue Historic District** is the **Glessner House**, built in 1887, and the **Widow Clarke House**, the oldest house in the city of Chicago and one of the few homes to survive the great Chicago Fire.

Some historic Chicago gangster moments are recorded at the **American Police Center and Museum** just northwest of the Prairie Avenue district on S. State Street. The museum's Gangster Alley has photographs of such notorious types as Al Capone, a model of a real jail cell, and an electric chair. There is also a display of hundreds of police shields and badges.

9. Science, Sojourner, and the South Side

The **Hyde Park/Kenwood** area of Chicago is only a few miles by car, bus, or train from the Prairie Avenue district, the Field Museum, or McCormick Place.

This south side section of the city is home to the switch flippingest, button pushingest, handle turningest, lever liftingest museum in the world. Not to mention home to one of Chicago's most successfully racially integrated neighborhoods, the world's first controlled self-sustaining chain reaction, and one of the world's most prestigious universities.

The **Museum of Science and Industry**, located in **Jackson Park**, was originally built as part of a world's fair called the World's Columbian Exposition of 1893. The museum officially opened in 1933 and is visited by more than four million people a year. Like the Field Museum, the Museum of Science and Industry is gigantic, so don't expect to see everything in one visit.

Some must-sees are the real German submarine, the U-505 captured during World War II (you can see Lake Michigan from the boat's periscope), and the coal mine, where you'll drop down 50 feet into what seems to be the real thing. Near the coal mine exit is Colleen Moore's Fairy Castle Doll House, complete with solid gold dishes, a "bear skin" rug with teeth from a mouse, and the world's smallest Bible, printed in

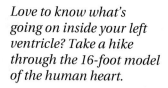

Love to know what's going on inside your left ventricle? Take a hike through the 16-foot model of the human heart.

1840. Kids Starway is the first museum exhibit that explores the emotional health of children.

At the Henry Crown Space Center, slip into some 3-D shades and blast off in the simulated space shuttle ride. You'll forget you are in the museum, in the city of Chicago, and even on the planet Earth.

Make sure you step into the OmniMax Theater and hold onto your seat while you watch films like *To Fly*, a movie that lets you feel what it's actually like to fly. You might also want to hold onto your stomach for this one.

If you lost your appetite, you'll get it back again after visiting the Food for Life Exhibit, complete with scrumptious displays of fake food, a fitness center, and an incubator full of hatching chickens. You'll find out what all those milk shakes and french fries are doing to you.

If you're ready for a salad, try the Century Room, or if you still have a hankering for hot dogs, try the Main Street Cafe, or how about, "I scream, you scream, we all scream for ice cream," which is what you'll scream at Finnegan's Ice Cream Parlor.

Not far from the museum at the **University of Chicago** campus stands the **Robie House**, designed by Frank Lloyd Wright and considered one of the most outstanding American homes built in the twentieth century.

Still mad for mummies? Walk one block west of the Robie House and you'll find the **Oriental Institute**, where at the back of the first big hall you'll find several mummies, a huge sculpture of King Tut, and scary skeletons.

These skeletons aren't half as scary as *Nuclear Energy*, Henry Moore's 12-ton sculpture commemorating the site where man first harnessed nuclear energy. The first self-sustained nuclear chain reaction took place on December 2, 1942, at 3:25 p.m. under what used to be the Stagg Field Grandstands and is now a library.

Just west of here is the **Du Sable Museum of African-American History** on E. 56th Place where you can find out about the lives of famous African-Americans like Frederick Douglass, Sojourner Truth, Malcolm X, and Martin Luther King, Jr. The museum has special workshops for children on topics like African mask making, the Kwanzaa celebration, and the Haitian carnival. The multimedia center has a library full of films and jazz recordings. The gift shop offers books on black theater, maps of Africa, and coloring books.

The Du Sable Museum sits in **Washington Park**, a great place for sledding in the winter and picnicking in the summer.

If you didn't bring your lunch and you didn't eat at the Museum of Science and Industry, try a famous Chicago pan or stuffed pizza at **Edwardo's** on E. 57th Street or have a bowl of chili on E. 53rd Street at **Mellow Yellow**, a winner in Chicago's Taste Fest. If you yearn for tofu and nori, then stop in at the **Sunflower Seed Health Food Store** at Harper Court. Next door, find toys galore at **Toys Et Cetera**. For a good read, hit the **Powell Bookstore** on E. 57th and Harper. **57th Street Books** on E. 57th and Kimbark has one of the biggest children's sections in the city. In between chapters catch a cup of hot chocolate at the **Medici** on E. 57th.

By now, you might think you've seen all there is to see in Chicago, but you've only just begun. Did you know Chicago is made up of more than 75 neighborhoods? You'll never be able to see them all in one visit, but the next chapter covers some of the highlights that shouldn't be missed.

10. Fortune Cookies and Fried Eel (Ethnic Neighborhoods)

Don't miss Chinatown on the near south side of Chicago.

Photo courtesy of Rustam Tahir/Chicago Office of Tourism

The Chinese believe that a doorway or a gate painted red brings good luck, health, and happiness.

From the days of Du Sable, people from around the globe have come to make a life for themselves in Chicago. People from Ireland, Germany, Poland, Italy, Greece, Lithuania, China, Vietnam, Africa, Mexico, and everywhere else you can think of have settled in Chicago's neighborhoods. The ethnic populations of these areas continue to grow and change from generation to generation. Some of these neighborhoods are within walking distance of the downtown area; most are a bus, car, or "L" ride away. Give yourself plenty of time to sightsee. Don't try to visit Rogers Park and Pilsen in the same day. But if you want to try dim sum, or see intricately colored Easter eggs, or buy silks from India, get ready to explore some more.

Did you ever see a Chinese telephone booth? Or how about street signs and shop signs written in Chinese? As you enter **Chinatown** (just a couple of miles south of the Loop), make sure you walk through the Gate of Happiness for good luck.

Tins of teas, jade Buddhas, dried seaweed, plum candy, Chinese/English calculators, Chinese hats, and Crazy Mix line the shelves at the **Mei Wah Company** on S. Wentworth. You'll really go crazy in **Bang, Bang**, a store filled with Chinese yoyos, flutes, clothes for kids, and a

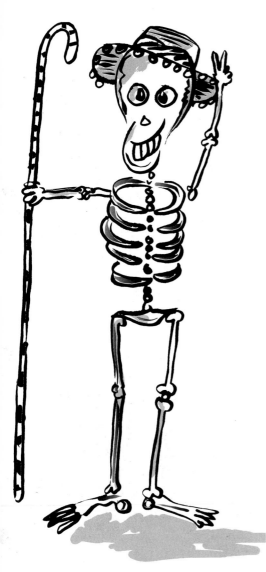

Día de los Muertos means "Day of the Dead." It is a day on which Mexican people honor their dead relatives with song, dance, food, and festivities. They believe dead folks appreciate the hullabaloo.

whole assortment of toys from China. The **Happy Garden Bakery** sells mountains of fortune cookies as well as other Chinese baked goods.

A visit to Chinatown is not complete without a Chinese meal. There are several restaurants from which to choose. The most popular is **Three Happiness** on W. Cermak. A good alternative if the Three Happiness is too crowded is the **Chiam Restaurant** on S. Wentworth, where you can try everything from dynamite dim sum to moo shu pork.

Burritos are the Mexican version of moo shu. Instead of a thin pancake wrapped around shredded vegetables and pork, this is a flour tortilla hugging a bunch of beans or any combination of beans, chili, cheese, and meat. While walking through **Pilsen** (on the Near Southwest Side), formerly a Czechoslovakian area, now Chicago's mostly Mexican neighborhood, notice the smell of tortillas filling the air. On the streets, kids kick soccer balls and call out to each other in Spanish.

The **Mexican Fine Arts Center Museum** holds the largest Día de los Muertos celebration in the country. So if you're there during the festivities (beginning of October through the end of November), dance, sing, and party down! Try a taco, a burrito, or an enchilada at Nuevo Leon on W. 18th, one of Pilsen's best Mexican restaurants. The food's great and inexpensive.

A historically important area is the Near West Side. Jane Addams moved into this overcrowded and poor neighborhood in 1889 and started **Hull House** on S. Halsted Street, a settlement house with public baths (many people couldn't afford to have private showers), playgrounds, a theater, a kitchen, and other facilities for the area's poor. Two of the settlement's original buildings remain. These buildings were turned into a museum where you can see Jane Addams's office, maps of the settlement, and a photograph of Addams herself.

A few blocks south you'll find the **Maxwell Street Market** (at Halsted and 14th sts.), the city's biggest flea market, where you can find absolutely anything from blenders to blintzes and pork chop sandwiches. Here on Sunday mornings, you can hear real Chicago Blues bands playing on street corners for free. Musicians often sell cassettes of their music.

North of there at Randolph and Desplaines streets sits **Haymarket Square**, scene of the 1886 worker's riot, where a bomb exploded and killed several policemen and civilians. This area is more peaceful now and is home to some good Jewish, Greek, and Italian restaurants. Try a corned beef sandwich at **Manny's Coffee Shop** on S. Jefferson or some pizza at **Gennaro's** on Taylor. Or at the **Parthenon** on S. Halsted, try saganaki, a flaming cheese dish. As the waiter serves the saganaki and douses the flames with a squirt of lemon juice, you and your friends can shout "Opa!" Another place for great Greek cuisine is the **Greek Islands**, just off S. Halsted.

Want something sweet? Try some incredibly edibly scrumptious sticky buns at **Ann Sathers** on N. Clark in **Andersonville** (on the North Side), Chicago's Swedish neighborhood. The **Swedish Museum**, also on N. Clark, has a listing of special events for kids that include basket-making and Swedish harvest celebrations.

Looking for a traditional Vietnamese celebration, complete with a dragon dance, music, and outdoor lanterns? During the Chinese New Year, which usually takes place sometime in January or February and lasts about 15 days, visit Chicago's New Chinatown (south of Anderson-

ville), home to many Vietnamese immigrants. At the Viet Hoa Market, see live crabs, squid, and huge eels.

South of here catch a fly ball at **Wrigleyville's** famous home of the Chicago Cubs, **Wrigley Field**. These baby bears are loved by their fans. Near Wrigley Field, bat your own balls in the batting cages at **Sluggers**, a game room with over 40 sport-related activities.

Wrigley Field is the home of the Chicago Cubs.

Photo courtesy of Peter J. Schultz/City of Chicago

If eel makes you squeal, grab a hot dog at **Fluky's** in **Rogers Park**, Chicago's northernmost neighborhood, where they give kids things like bubble gum in the shape of hot dogs and moon monster rings. The markets on Devon Avenue are filled with all kinds of East Indian items, everything from spices to silk saris. Try some curried chicken, basmati rice, and alou gohbi. Remember, Indian food is spicy. Cool off with a magical mango shake at the **Gandhi India Restaurant**.

If sports are your sport, you already know Chicago is famous for more than just baseball and football. The **Chicago Black Hawks***, who take their name from the famous Indian chief, not the birds, whack that little puck around from mid-October to mid-April at the Chicago Stadium. Another beloved bunch of Chicago animals are the* **Chicago Bulls***. Michael "Air" Jordan and the rest of the team slam dunk their way through basketball season at the same stadium.*

The National Hot Dog and Sausage Council says that 80 percent of all people who go to baseball games eat hot dogs.

Chicago has the biggest Polish population outside of Warsaw, Poland, as well as the biggest Lithuanian population outside of Lithuania.

For some real magic, check out **Magic, Inc**. on N. Lincoln in the area called **Ravenswood** or **Lincoln Square** (on the Northwest Side). Let Bruce, the resident magician, pull some coins or maybe a flower out of your ear.

Two museums off the beaten track (on the Near Northwest Side) which shouldn't be missed if you're cruising nearby are the **Polish Museum** on N. Milwaukee, full of model ships and painted Easter eggs, and the **Ukrainian National Museum** on W. Chicago Avenue, where you'll see more intricately painted eggs and hear stories of ancient Ukrainian culture.

Another-out-of-the-way museum but one worth visiting on the Near West Side is the **Museum of Holography** on W. Washington, where you'll say to yourself, "No, that can't be a real cat inside that picture." You won't believe your eyes as you marvel at two-dimensional pictures that appear as three-dimensional objects.

The Lithuanian village and the medieval room at the **Balzekas Museum of Lithuanian Culture** are designed with children in mind. This museum in West Lawn, on the Southwest Side, has a replica of an old Lithuanian village, armor, and puppet shows.

11. The Outer Limits (Chicago's Suburbs)

Kids travel to and explore far away lands on a Phoenician sailing ship at the Kohl Children's Museum.

Photo courtesy of Kohl Children's Museum

Chicago has still more in store for you. To see some Midwest hot spots, you'll have to venture far and wide outside the city limits to some of Chicago's great suburban sights. You will need to travel by train, car, or bus. The following places are in Chicago's north and west suburbs.

Ever want to see yourself as a glamour girl in a glittering golden gown, high heels, and pearls? Or chief of a famous hospital? Or maybe an airline pilot? At the **Kohl Children's Museum** in Wilmette (one of Chicago's North Shore suburbs), dress up and be a star in your own videotaped TV show.

*Getting ready to leave Chicago? If you're flying, consider a tour of **O'Hare Airport**, the busiest airport in the world. If your plane departs from **Midway,** you'll take off from an airport that sits right in the middle of the city. Traveling by train? Look around **Union Station**, just west of the Sears Tower and see where the movie,* The Untouchables, *was filmed.*

Wear crazy face paints, float inside your own kid-sized soap bubble at the Human Bubble Exhibit, and shop at a miniature grocery store, but don't try to eat the food—it's all fake! Kohl's mini Jewel/Osco food market is an exact kid-sized replica of a real supermarket.

Sail on a Venetian sailing ship at "Long Ago and Far Away," an ancient royal kingdom from 1000 B.C.

At Kohl's Learning Store, you'll find a great assortment of dinosaur books, crystal-growing sets, rocket ships, and doll-making kits.

From here, feast on fabulous flapjacks at the nearby Original Pancake House on Green Bay Road. This well-known Chicago area landmark also serves hefty hamburgers, sandwiches, gyros, and delicious desserts.

Not far from here is the famous **Bahai House of Worship**, which looks like a huge orange juice squeezer and is definitely worth a peek if you are on your way to an outdoor summer concert at the **Ravinia Festival** (north of Wilmette) in the Chicago suburb of Highland Park. Ravinia's season runs from May through September and offers all kinds of concerts featuring everything from the Chicago Symphony to dance companies and special young people's music programs.

Buildings, concrete, buses, trains, noise, and people can be exhausting. If the city scene's got you screaming for trees and trails, take a hike through the **Morton Arboretum** (in Lisle, a town west of Chicago), sniff some snapdragons at the **Chicago Botanic Garden** in Glencoe (just north of the city and south of Ravinia), or walk through the wilds of **Brookfield Zoo** (west of the city), where you can see a dolphin show. **Oak Park** is not far from the zoo and is due west of downtown Chicago. Here you can visit Frank Lloyd Wright's home and studio.

12. Wave Good-bye to the Windy City

Now that you've been to the top of the world, ridden the L, eaten dim sum, heard the blues, bought T-shirts and postcards, cruised the river and the lake, traveled in space, batted a ball or two, and maybe even flown a kite in one of the Windy City's windiest parks, it's time to move on.

Surely, your trip has been a breeze, but even if you got on the wrong train or didn't like the taste of grilled eel, you probably realize you've learned oodles of new things.

Traveling is the greatest way to try exotic foods, hear foreign languages, understand different cultures, and even make new friends.

Maybe you've kept a written log of your adventures, taken photographs, or even drawn some pictures. However you've chosen to preserve your multitude of memories, you've had tons of fun. Don't worry if you didn't get to see everything; remember, you can always come back to that great, second to none, midwestern metropolis, your kind of town—Chicago!

Events in the Windy City

January
Cubs Fan Convention
  Wrigley Field
  312-951-CUBS
University of Chicago Folk Festival
  312-702-9793

February
Azalea and Camellia Show
  Lincoln Park and Garfield Park Conservatories
  312-294-2493
Black History Month
  Chicago Public Library Cultural Center and the
  Du Sable Museum of African American History
  312-947-0600
Chicago Auto Show
  McCormick Place
  312-698-6630
Chinese New Year Parade
  Wentworth Avenue and Cermak Road
  312-326-5607

March
Lithuanian Easter Egg Decorating Workshops
and Display
  312-582-6500
Maple Syrup Festival
  312-583-8970
Medinah Shrine Circus
  Crippled Children's Hospital
  312-266-5000
St. Patrick's Day Parade
  The Loop
  312-744-4691

April
Brookfield Zoo Easter Parade and Bonnet
Contest
  312-242-2630
Chicago Cubs opening day
  Wrigley Field
  312-878-2827

Chicago Latino Film Festival
  312-327-3184
Chicago White Sox opening day
  Comiskey Park
  312-924-1000
International Theater Festival of Chicago
  312-664-3370
Spring and Easter Flower Show
  Lincoln Park and Garfield Park Conservatories
  312-294-2493

May
Buckingham Fountain Display
  Grant Park at Congress and Lake Shore Dr.
Chicago International Art Exposition
  Navy Pier
  312-787-6858
Chicago International Festival of Flowers and
Gardens
  312-787-6858
Greek Independence Day Parade
  312-787-6858
Polish Constitution Day Parade
  312-286-0500
Walk with Israel
  312-675-2200

June
57th Street Art Fair
  the block bounded by 56th and 57th streets and
  Kenwood and Kimbark avenues
Body Politic Street Festival
  312-871-3000 or 348-7901
Brandeis University Used Book Sale
  312-446-6177
Chicago Blues Festival
  Petrillo Music Shell
  312-744-3315
Chicago Book and Memorabilia Fair
  Dearborn Street
  312-663-1595

Chicago Gospel Festival
  Petrillo Music Shell
  312-744-3315
Latino Film Festival
  Getz Theater of Columbia College
  312-327-3184
Old Town Art Fair
  312-337-5962

July
Air and Water Show
  North Avenue Beach
  312-294-2494
Fourth of July Celebrations
  Grant Park
  312-294-2420
Greek Festival
  St. Andrew's Greek Orthodox Church
  312-334-4515
Howard Street Alive!
  312-508-5885
Neighborhood festivals
  Mayor's Office of Special Events
  312-744-3315
Sheffield Garden Walk and Festival
  312-327-4148
Taste of Chicago
  Grant Park
  312-744-3315
Taste of Lincoln Avenue
  312-472-9046

August
Broadway Art Fair
  312-248-8285
Chicago Jazz Festival
  Petrillo Music Shell
  312-744-3135
Chicago RiverFest
  312-922-4020
Medieval Fair in Oz Park
  312-880-5200
Venetian Night
  Monroe Street Harbor to the Planetarium
  312-294-2200
  312-744-3315

September
Chicago International Folk Fair
  312-744-3315
Chicago International New Art Forms
Exposition
  Navy Pier
  312-787-6858
Mexican Independence Day Parade
  The Loop
  312-674-5838

October
Chicago International Antiques Show
  Navy Pier
  312-787-6858
Chicago International Film Festival
  312-644-3400
Columbus Day Parade
  312-372-6788
Dinosaur Days
  Field Museum
  312-922-9410
Morton Arboretum Bonsai Society Show
  312-968-0074
Multimedia's Chicago International Festival of
Children's Films
  312-281-9075
Ringling Bros. & Barnum & Bailey Circus
  Chicago Stadium
  312-733-5300

November
Arts Expressions
  312-895-5300
Christmas Around the World
  Museum of Science and Industry
  312-684-1414
Christmas Tree Lighting
  Daley Center Plaza
Chrysanthemum Show
  Garfield Park and Lincoln Park Conservatories
  312-533-1281
Lithuanian Christmas Straw Ornament
Workshops
  Balzekas Museum of Lithuanian Culture
  312-582-6500
Veterans Day Parade
  312-744-3515

December
A Christmas Carol
  Goodman Theater
  312-443-3800
Brookfield Zoo's Christmas Party
  Children's Zoo
  312-242-2630
Christmas Flower Show
  Lincoln Park and Garfield Park Conservatories
  312-294-2493
In the Spirit
  Chicago Public Library Cultural Center
  312-346-3278
Nutcracker Ballet
  Arie Crown Theater
  312-791-6000

Appendix

Adler Planetarium
1300 S. Lake Shore Dr.
312-322-0300
Handicapped Access

American Police Center & Museum
1705-25 S. State St.
312-431-0005

Art Institute of Chicago
410 S. Michigan Ave.
312-443-3600
Children's tours 312-443-3688
Handicapped Access

Balzekas Museum of Lithuanian Culture
6500 S. Pulaski Rd.
312-582-6500

Bicycle Chicago Rental
804 W. Randolph
312-738-9754

Brookfield Zoo
8400 W. 31st
Brookfield
312-242-2630

Bureau of Traffic
Engineering and Operations
320 N. Clark St., Rm. 402
312-744-4684

Chicago Academy of Sciences
2001 N. Clark St.
312-871-2668

Chicago Architecture Foundation
224 S. Michigan Ave.
312-922-3432

Chicago Board of Trade
LaSalle at Jackson
312-435-3625
or 312-435-3590

Chicago Board Options Exchange
400 S. LaSalle
312-786-5600

Chicago Botanic Garden
Lake Cook Rd.
Glencoe
708-835-5440

Chicago City Hall-Cook County Bldg.
121 North LaSalle
312-443-5500

Chicago Historical Society
1601 N. Clark St.
312-642-4600
Handicapped Access

Chicago Mercantile Exchange
30 S. Wacker Dr.
312-930-1000

Chicago Park District
425 McFetridge Dr.
312-294-2200

Chicago Stadium
(Bulls & Black Hawks)
1800 W. Madison
312-733-5300

Chicago Symphony Orchestra
220 S. Michigan
312-435-6666

Chicago Tourism Council
163 E. Pearson St.
312-280-5740

Chicago Tribune's Freedom Center
777 W. Chicago Ave.
312-222-2116

Children's Theater of Second City
1616 Wells St.
312-337-3992

City of Chicago
Department of Water
Tours, call 312-744-7007

City of Chicago Store
435 E. Illinois
312-467-1111

Comiskey Park
(White Sox)
333 W. 35th St.
312-924-1000

CTA Bus Information
W. Merchandise Mart Plaza
312-664-7200

Du Sable Museum of African History
5700 S. Cottage Grove
312-947-0600
Handicapped Access

Chicago Children's Museum
435 E. Illinois St.
312-527-1000
Handicapped Access

Field Museum of Natural History
S. Lake Shore Dr. at
E. Roosevelt Rd.
312-922-9410
Handicapped Access

Glessner House
1800 S. Prairie
312-922-3432

Grant Park
  Soldier Field Stadium
  16th St. & the Lake
  312-294-2200
  Abraham Lincoln Monument
  Congress Dr. between
  Michigan Ave. & Columbus
  Dr.

Grant Park Concerts
James C. Petrillo Music Shell
E. Jackson & Columbus Dr.
312-294-2420

John Hancock Center Observatory
875 N. Michigan Ave.
312-751-3681

Here's Chicago
163 E. Pearson
312-467-7114

Hull House
800 S. Halsted
312-413-5353

Hystopolis Puppet Theatre
Free Street Community
Arts Center
441 W. North Blvd.
312-787-7387

Illinois State Tourist Information Center
806 N. Michigan Ave.
312-280-5740

Kohl Children's Museum
165 Green Bay Road
Wilmette
708-251-7781 or
708-256-6056

Lincoln Park
2045 Lincoln Park West
312-294-4750
Conservatory
  Fullerton & Stockton Dr.
  312-294-4770
Farm-in-the-Zoo
  312-294-4662
Theater on the Lake
  Fullerton & Lake Shore Dr.
  312-348-7075

Lincoln Park Bike & Roller-blade Rental
(at Cafe Brauer)
312-280-2727

Lincoln Park Paddleboat Rental
312-280-5151

Lincoln Park Zoo General Information
2200 N. Cannon Dr.
312-294-4660

McCormick Place
McCormick Pl. & Lake Shore Dr.
312-791-7500

Mexican Fine Arts Center Museum
1852 W. 19th St.
312-738-1503

Morton Arboretum
Lisle
708-968-0074

Museum of Broadcast Communications
N./Michigan Ave. at
Washington
312-629-6000
Handicapped Access

Museum of Contemporary Art
237 E. Ontario St.
312-280-2660
Handicapped Access

Museum of Holography
1134 W. Washington St.
312-226-1007

Museum of Science and Industry
5700 Lake Shore Dr.
312-684-1414
Handicapped Access

North Pier
435 E. Illinois St.
312-440-8840

O'Hare Airport
Mannheim Road at
Kennedy Expwy
686-2200

The Oriental Institute
University of Chicago
1155 East 58th St.
312-702-9521

The Peace Museum
430 W. Erie St.
312-541-1474

Polish Museum of America
984 N. Milwaukee Ave.
312-384-3352

Ravinia Festival
1575 Oakwood
Highland Park
312-728-4642

Robie House
5757 S. Woodlawn Ave.
312-702-8374

Sears Tower Skydeck Observatory
233 S. Wacker
312-875-9696
Handicapped Access

John G. Shedd Aquarium
1200 S. Lake Shore Dr.
312-939-2438
Handicapped Access

Maurice Spertus Museum of Judaica
618 S. Michigan Ave.
312-922-9012

State of Illinois Center
100 W. Randolph St.

Swedish American Museum of Chicago
5211 N. Clark St.
312-728-8111

Terra Museum of American Art
666 N. Michigan Ave.
312-664-3939

Ukrainian National Museum
2453 W. Chicago Ave.
312-276-6565

Wacky Pirate Cruise
Mercury Dock
312-332-1366

Harold Washington Library Center
400 S. State St.
312-747-4999

Wendella Sightseeing Boat Tours
400 N. Michigan Ave.
312-337-1446

Widow Clarke House
1855 S. Indiana Ave.
312-326-1393

Wrigley Field
(Cubs)
1060 West Addison
312-404-2827 or
312-878-CUBS

62

Index

from John Muir Publications

Kidding Around Series
Family Travel Guides

All are 7"x 9", 64 pages, and $9.95 paperback except for *Kidding Around the National Parks* and *Kidding Around Spain*, which are 108 pages and $12.95.

Kidding Around Atlanta, 2nd ed.
Kidding Around Boston, 2nd ed.
Kidding Around Chicago, 2nd ed.
Kidding Around the Hawaiian Islands
Kidding Around London, 2nd ed.
Kidding Around Los Angeles
Kidding Around the National Parks
  of the Southwest
Kidding Around New York City, 2nd ed.
Kidding Around Paris, 2nd ed.
Kidding Around Philadelphia
Kidding Around San Diego
Kidding Around San Francisco
Kidding Around Santa Fe
Kidding Around Seattle
Kidding Around Spain
Kidding Around Washington, D.C., 2nd ed.

X-ray Vision Series

Each title in the series is 8½" x 11", 48 pages, and $9.95 paperback, with four-color photographs and illustrations. All are written by Ron Schultz.

Looking Inside the Brain
Looking Inside Cartoon Animation
Looking Inside Caves and Caverns
Looking Inside Sports Aerodynamics
Looking Inside Sunken Treasure
Looking Inside Telescopes and the
  Night Sky

Masters of Motion Series

Each title in the series is 10¼" x 9", 48 pages, and $9.95 paperback, with four-color photographs and illustrations.

How to Drive an Indy Race Car
How to Fly a 747
How to Fly the Space Shuttle

Rainbow Warrior Artists Series

Each title is written by Reavis Moore with a foreword by LeVar Burton and is 8½" x

11", 48 pages, $14.95 hardcover and $9.95 paperback, with color photographs and illustrations.

Native Artists of Africa
Native Artists of Europe
Native Artists of North America

Extremely Weird Series

All of the titles are written by Sarah Lovett, 8½" x 11", 48 pages, $9.95 paperback and $14.95 hardcover.

Extremely Weird Bats
Extremely Weird Birds
Extremely Weird Endangered Species
Extremely Weird Fishes
Extremely Weird Frogs
Extremely Weird Insects
Extremely Weird Mammals
Extremely Weird Micro Monsters
Extremely Weird Primates
Extremely Weird Reptiles
Extremely Weird Sea Creatures
Extremely Weird Snakes
Extremely Weird Spiders

Kids Explore Series

Each title is written by kids, for kids, by the Westridge Young Writers Workshop, 7" x 9", with photographs and illustrations by the kids.

Kids Explore America's African
  American Heritage
  128 pages, $9.95 paperback
Kids Explore America's Hispanic
  Heritage
  112 pages, $9.95 paperback
Kids Explore America's Japanese
  American Heritage
  144 pages, $9.95 paperback
Kids Explore the Gifts of Children With
  Special Needs
  128 pages, $9.95 paperback

Bizarre & Beautiful Series

Each title is 8½" x 11", 48 pages, $9.95 paperback and $14.95 hardcover, with four-color photographs and illustrations.

Bizarre & Beautiful Ears

Bizarre & Beautiful Eyes
Bizarre & Beautiful Feelers
Bizarre & Beautiful Noses
Bizarre & Beautiful Tongues

Rough and Ready Series

Each title is 48 pages, 8½" x 11", and $12.95 hardcover, with two-color illustrations and duotone archival photographs.

Rough and Ready Cowboys
Rough and Ready Homesteaders
Rough and Ready Loggers
Rough and Ready Outlaws and Lawmen
Rough and Ready Prospectors
Rough and Ready Railroaders

American Origins Series

Each title is 48 pages, 8½" x 11", $12.95 hardcover, with two-color illustrations and duotone archival photographs.

Tracing Our English Roots
Tracing Our German Roots
Tracing Our Irish Roots
Tracing Our Italian Roots
Tracing Our Japanese Roots
Tracing Our Jewish Roots
Tracing Our Polish Roots

Environmental Titles

Habitats: Where the Wild Things Live
8½" x 11", 48 pages, color illustrations, $9.95 paper

The Indian Way: Learning to
  Communicate with Mother Earth
7" x 9", 114 pages, two-color illustrations, $9.95 paper

Rads, Ergs, and Cheeseburgers: The Kids
  Guide to Energy and the Environment
7" x 9", 108 pages, two-color illustrations, $13.95 paper

The Kids' Environment Book: What's
  Awry and Why
7" x 9", 192 pages, two-color illustrations, $13.95 paper

Spanish

3

verde
green

tortuga
turtle

roca
rock

CARSON-DELLOSA®
PUBLISHING GROUP

Greensboro, NC 27425 USA

SO-AGP-887

Pronunciation Key

Use the pronunciation key below to learn how to say and make the sound of each Spanish letter.

Spanish Letter	English Pronunciation of Letter	The Sound the Letter Makes	Example of the Letter Sound
a	ah	ah	p<u>o</u>t
b	be	b	<u>b</u>at
c	say	k or s	<u>c</u>at, <u>c</u>ity
d	de	d	<u>d</u>og
e	eh	e	p<u>e</u>t
f	efe	f, ph	<u>f</u>oot
g	hey	g, h	<u>g</u>o, <u>h</u>and
h	ache	silent	silent
i	ee	ee	f<u>ee</u>t
j	hota	h	<u>h</u>ot
k	ka	k	ca<u>k</u>e
l	ele	l	<u>l</u>emon
m	eme	m	<u>m</u>ind
n	ene	n	<u>n</u>o
ñ	eñe	ñ	on<u>i</u>on
o	o	o	b<u>oa</u>t
p	pe	p	<u>p</u>ot
q	ku	ku	<u>c</u>ool
r	ere	r	<u>r</u>obe
s	ese	s	<u>s</u>o
t	te	t	<u>t</u>oe
u	oo	oo	p<u>oo</u>l
v	ve	v	<u>v</u>ine
w	doblay-oo	w	<u>w</u>e
x	equis	ks	e<u>x</u>it
y	ee griega	y	<u>y</u>ellow
z	seta	s	<u>s</u>uit

Note: The letters "t" and "d" are pronounced with the tongue slightly between the teeth and not behind the teeth.

Brighter Child®
An imprint of Carson-Dellosa Publishing LLC
P.O. Box 35665
Greensboro, NC 27425 USA

05-224197784

Table of Contents

Numbers Crossword

Use the words at the bottom to help you with this crossword puzzle. Write the Spanish number words in the puzzle spaces. Follow the English clues.

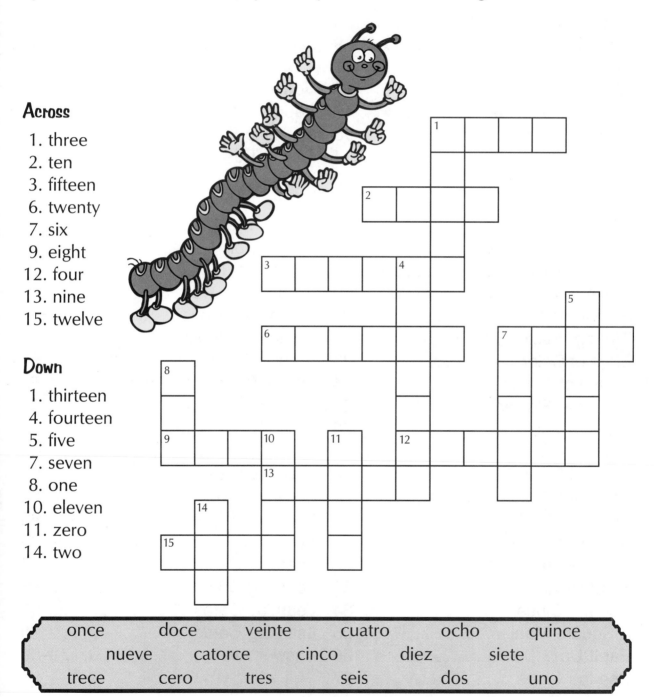

Across

1. three
2. ten
3. fifteen
6. twenty
7. six
9. eight
12. four
13. nine
15. twelve

Down

1. thirteen
4. fourteen
5. five
7. seven
8. one
10. eleven
11. zero
14. two

once	doce	veinte	cuatro	ocho	quince
nueve	catorce	cinco	diez	siete	
trece	cero	tres	seis	dos	uno

Numbers

After each numeral, write the number word in Spanish. Refer to the words below to help you.

Word Bank

veinte	cuatro	nueve	diez	diecisiete	quince
doce	once	trece	siete	uno	tres
catorce	dos	cero	ocho	cinco	dieciséis
diecinueve		dieciocho		seis	

0 _____   11 _____

1 _____   12 _____

2 _____   13 _____

3 _____   14 _____

4 _____   15 _____

5 _____   16 _____

6 _____   17 _____

7 _____   18 _____

8 _____   19 _____

9 _____   20 _____

10 _____

Numbers Illustration

Write the number. Draw that many things in the box. The first one is done for you.

☆☆☆☆ ☆☆☆☆ **ocho** means __8__	**cinco** means _____	**diecisiete** means _____
doce means _____	**uno** means _____	**dos** means _____
catorce means _____	**nueve** means _____	**veinte** means _____
siete means _____	**cuatro** means _____	**quince** means _____

Who Is It?

Write the names of people you may know that fit each description below.

tú–informal or familiar form of you	
someone you refer to by first name	
your sister or brother (or cousin)	
a classmate	
a close friend	
a child younger than yourself	

usted–formal or polite form of you	
someone with a title	
an older person	
a stranger	
a person of authority	

How would you speak to each person below? Write *tú* or *usted* after each person named.

1. Dr. Hackett _____
2. Susana _____
3. a four-year-old _____
4. your grandfather _____
5. the governor _____

6. your best friend _____
7. your sister _____
8. the principal _____
9. a classmate _____
10. a stranger _____

Masculine and Feminine

All Spanish nouns and adjectives have gender. This means they are either masculine or feminine. Here are two basic rules to help determine the gender of words. There are other rules for gender which you will learn as you study more Spanish.

1. Spanish words ending in -o are usually masculine.
2. Spanish words ending in -a are usually feminine.

Write the following words in the charts to determine their gender. Write the English meanings to the right. Use a Spanish-English dictionary if you need help.

maestra	libro	escritorio	negro	abrigo	sopa	tienda
amigo	ventana	pluma	maestro	vestido	fruta	museo
silla	puerta	anaranjado	amiga	camisa	queso	casa
rojo	cuaderno	blanco	falda	chaqueta		

Masculine		Feminine	
words ending in -o	meaning of the word	words ending in -a	meaning of the word

It's a Small World

In Spanish, there are four ways to say "the"—*el, la, los,* and *las.* The definite article (the) agrees with its noun in gender (masculine or feminine) and number (singular or plural).

Masculine singular nouns go with *el.* Feminine singular nouns go with *la.*

Examples: *el libro* (the book)   *el papel* (the paper)
                    la silla (the chair)   *la regla* (the ruler)

Masculine plural nouns go with *los.* Feminine plural nouns go with *las.*

Examples: *los libros* (the books)   *los papeles* (the papers)
                    las sillas (the chairs)   *las reglas* (the rulers)

Refer to the Word Bank to complete the chart. Write the singular and plural forms and the correct definite articles. The first ones have been done for you.

Word Bank	cuaderno	mesa	pluma	oso	falda
	papel	gato	bota	silla	libro

English	Masculine Singular	Masculine Plural
the book	el libro	los libros
the paper		
the notebook		
the cat		
the bear		

English	Feminine Singular	Feminine Plural
the chair	la silla	las sillas
the table		
the boot		
the skirt		
the pen		

Pretty Colors

Adjectives are words that tell about or describe nouns. Color each box as indicated in Spanish. Use a Spanish-English dictionary if you need help.

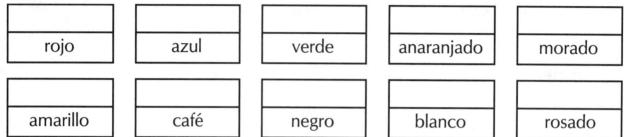

| | rojo | | azul | | verde | | anaranjado | | morado |

| | amarillo | | café | | negro | | blanco | | rosado |

Here are some new adjectives. Copy the Spanish adjectives in the boxes. Write the Spanish words next to the English at the bottom of the page.

bonita	pretty	feo	ugly
grande	big	pequeño	small
limpio	clean	sucio	dirty
viejo	old	nuevo	new
alegre	happy	triste	sad

old _____   pretty _____   sad _____

big _____   small _____   happy _____

new _____   dirty _____   ugly _____

clean _____

Words to Describe

Descriptive adjectives are words that describe nouns. Refer to the Word Bank to write the Spanish adjective that describes each picture.

Word Bank

alegre	grande	nuevo	pequeño	feo	rico
limpio	sucio	bonita	triste	viejo	pobre
alto	bajo	abierto	cerrado		

large	new	ugly	happy
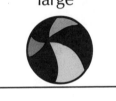			

old	sad	small	clean
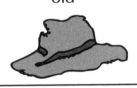		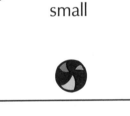	

pretty	dirty	tall	open
		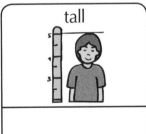	

rich	short	closed	poor
	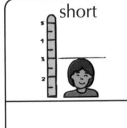		

Spanish: Grade 3

Words to Describe

Write the Spanish words for the clue words in the crossword puzzle.

Across

3. poor
7. open
9. tall
11. clean
12. dirty
13. new

Down

1. ugly
2. closed
4. happy
5. pretty
6. large
8. old
10. sad

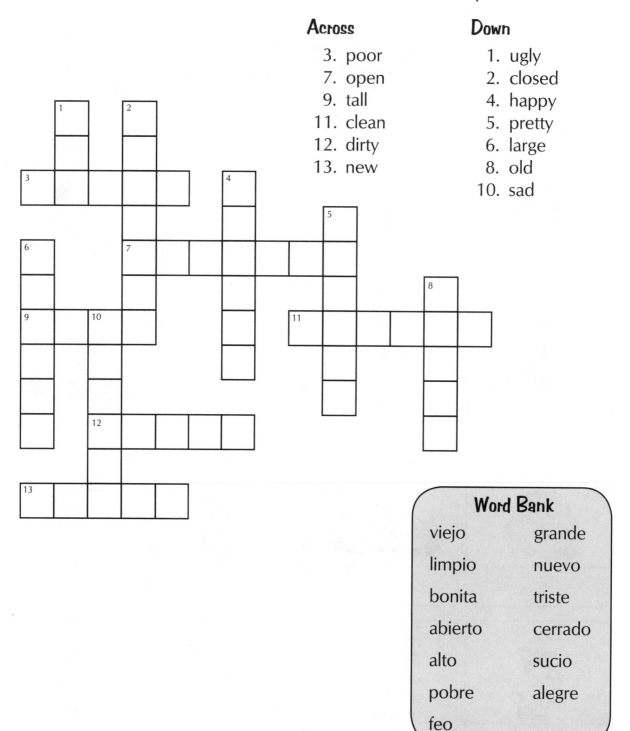

Word Bank

viejo	grande
limpio	nuevo
bonita	triste
abierto	cerrado
alto	sucio
pobre	alegre
feo	

Action Words

In each box, copy the Spanish action verb. Then, write the English word below it.

comer

_____

_____

beber

_____

_____

dormir

_____

_____

tocar

_____

_____

hablar

_____

_____

limpiar

_____

_____

mirar

_____

_____

dar

_____

_____

Word Bank

to touch	to look at	to eat	to give
to drink	to speak	to clean	to sleep

13

Spanish: Grade 3

Action Figures

Write the Spanish words from the Word Bank that fit in these word blocks.
Write the English below the blocks.

1.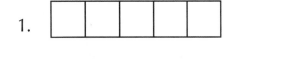

_____

2.

_____

3.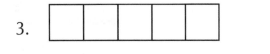

_____

4.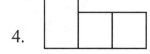

_____

5.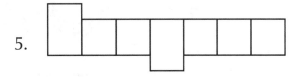

_____

6.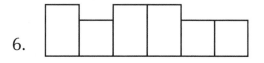

_____

7.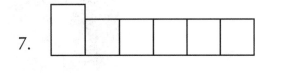

_____

8.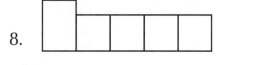

_____

Greetings Paste Up

Cut out a picture from a magazine that shows the meaning of each greeting and glue it next to the correct word or words.

¡Hola!

¿Cómo te llamas?

Me llamo...

¿Cómo estás?

bien

mal

así, así

¡Adiós!

What's Your Name?

Word Bank

I'm so-so.	What's your name?	I'm well/fine.
I'm ____ years old.	I'm not doing well.	My name is ___.
I'm not well.	How are you?	How old are you?

Refer to the Word Bank to translate the Spanish questions and answers into English.

1. ¿Cómo te llamas? _____

    Me llamo _____. _____

2. ¿Cómo estás? _____

    Estoy bien/mal/así así. _____

3. ¿Cuántos años tienes? _____

    Tengo ___ años. _____

Word Bank

hello	please	friend	yes
no	thank you	goodbye	See you later!

Write the English meaning after the Spanish word.

4. hola _____

5. amigo, amiga _____

6. sí _____

7. no _____

8. por favor _____

9. gracias _____

10. ¡Hasta luego! _____

11. adiós _____

Word Blocks

Write the Spanish words from the Word Bank that fit in these word blocks.
Don't forget the punctuation. Write the English meanings below the blocks.

1.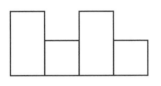

2.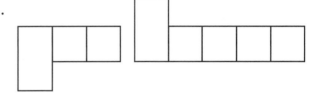

3.

4.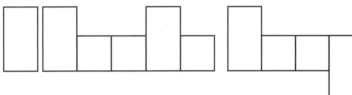

5.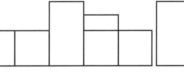

6.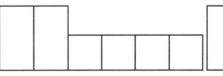

7.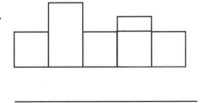

Spanish Word Bank

por favor	adiós	Estoy bien.
hola	¡Hasta luego!	¿Cómo te llamas?
no	¿Cómo estás?	

8.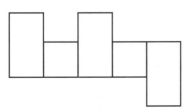

Greetings

Write the English meaning of the Spanish words and phrases.

1. señor _____

2. señora _____

3. señorita _____

4. maestro _____

5. maestra _____

6. ¡Buenos días! _____

7. ¡Buenas tardes! _____

8. ¡Buenas noches! _____

9. Vamos a contar. _____

Word Bank

Mr.	Good night!	Good morning!
Good afternoon!	teacher (female)	teacher (male)
Miss	Let's count.	Mrs.

Draw a picture to show the time of day that you use each expression.

¡Buenos días!	¡Buenas tardes!	¡Buenas noches!

Spanish Greetings

Write the Spanish word for each clue in the crossword puzzle.

Across

1. bad
4. good
7. teacher (male)
9. friend (female)
10. Mr.
11. Miss

Down

2. friend (male)
3. hello
5. thank you
6. goodbye
7. teacher (female)
8. Mrs.

Word Bank

amiga	mal
señora	señor
maestra	bien
adiós	hola
señorita	gracias
amigo	maestro

Yesterday and Today

Write the Spanish words for the days of the week. Remember, in Spanish-speaking countries, Monday is the first day of the week.

Word Bank

miércoles	lunes	sábado
viernes	domingo	martes
jueves		

Monday   _____

Tuesday   _____

Wednesday   _____

Thursday   _____

Friday   _____

Saturday   _____

Sunday   _____

If today is Monday, yesterday was Sunday. Complete the following chart by identifying the missing days in Spanish. The first one is done for you.

ayer (yesterday)	hoy (today)	mañana (tomorrow)
martes	miércoles	jueves
lunes		
		sábado
	domingo	
	jueves	
		martes
viernes		

Rain in April

Refer to the Word Bank to write the Spanish word for the given month. Then, in the box, draw a picture of something that happens in that month of the year. Remember that Spanish months do not begin with capital letters.

Word Bank

agosto	septiembre	noviembre	mayo
junio	enero	octubre	febrero
marzo	julio	diciembre	abril

January _____		July _____	
February _____		August _____	
March _____		September _____	
April _____		October _____	
May _____		November _____	
June _____		December _____	

Writing Practice

Copy the following paragraph in your best handwriting. Practice reading it out loud.

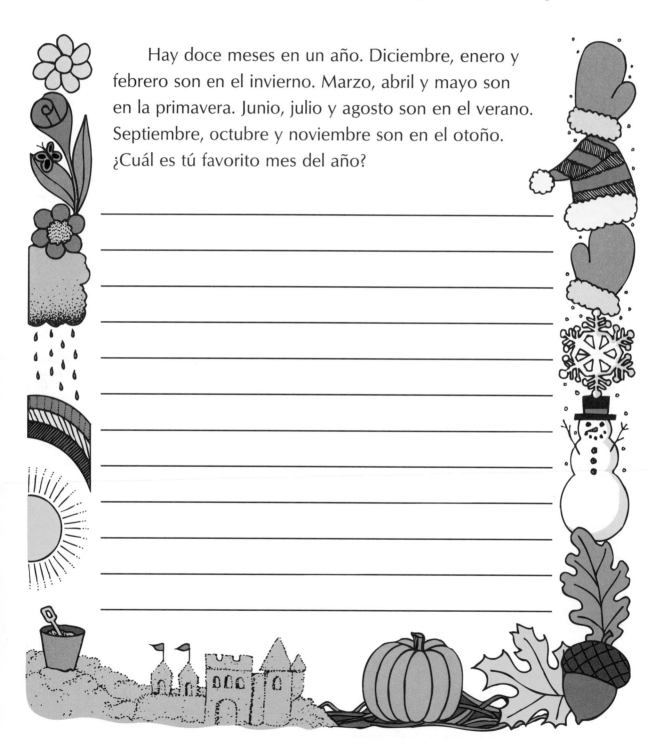

Hay doce meses en un año. Diciembre, enero y febrero son en el invierno. Marzo, abril y mayo son en la primavera. Junio, julio y agosto son en el verano. Septiembre, octubre y noviembre son en el otoño. ¿Cuál es tú favorito mes del año?

Birds of Color

Color the birds according to the words listed.

23

House of Colors

Color each crayon with the correct color for the Spanish word. Add something with your favorite color.

☐ rojo ☐ negro ☐ café ☐ rosado
☐ azul ☐ amarillo ☐ blanco ☐ verde

Color the Flowers

Color each flower with the correct color for the Spanish word.

☐ azul   ☐ café   ☐ amarillo   ☐ rosado
☐ verde   ☐ rojo   ☐ morado   ☐ anaranjado

Moving Colors

Color the pictures according to the words listed.

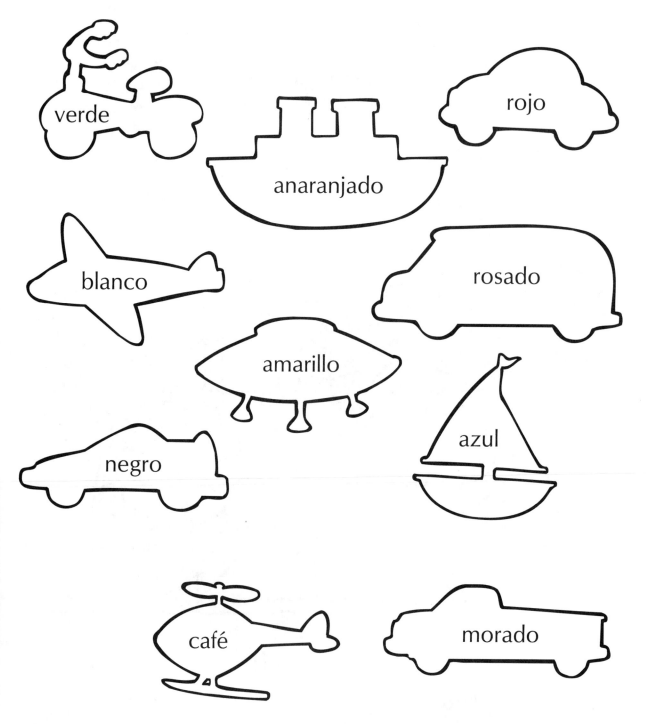

verde

anaranjado

rojo

blanco

rosado

amarillo

azul

negro

café

morado

What is your favorite color? (Answer in Spanish.) _____

Color Crossword

Write the correct Spanish color words in the spaces.
Follow the English color clues.

Across

3. yellow
5. purple
6. black
8. white
10. pink

Down

1. blue
2. red
4. orange
7. green
9. brown

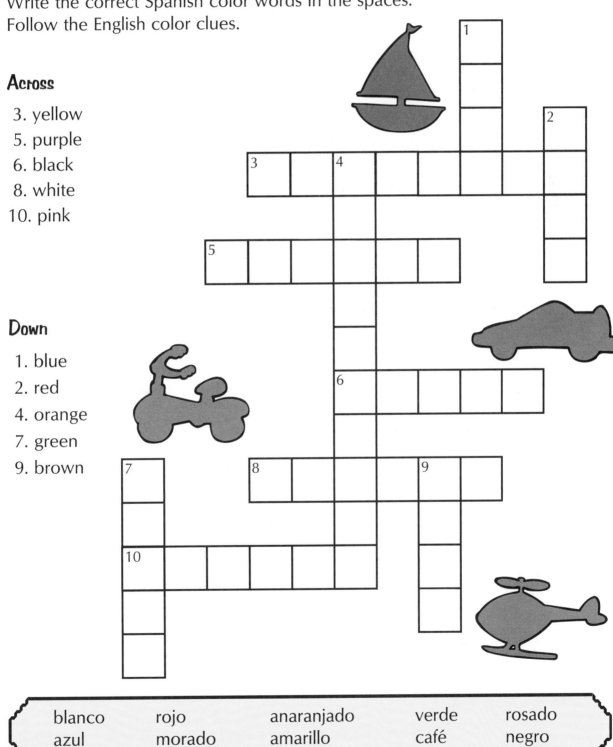

| blanco | rojo | anaranjado | verde | rosado |
| azul | morado | amarillo | café | negro |

Colorful Flowers

Color the flowers according to the Spanish color words shown.

azul

amarillo

morado

rosado

blanco

anaranjado

verde

verde

verde

rojo

negro

de color café

Draw and Color

In each box, write the Spanish color word. Use the Word Bank below to help you. Then, draw and color a picture of something that is usually that color.

rojo	*anaranjado*	*café*
red is _____	orange is _____	brown is _____
azul	*morado*	*negro*
blue is _____	purple is _____	black is _____
verde	*amarillo*	*rosado*
green is _____	yellow is _____	pink is _____

Which Spanish color from the Word Bank is not used above? *blanco*

Word Bank

blanco	morado	verde	rosado
azul	anaranjado	café	negro
rojo	amarillo		

Butterfly Garden

Color the butterfly garden as indicated in Spanish.

Across the Spectrum

Write the Spanish for each clue word in the crossword puzzle.

Across

2. blue
4. brown
6. red
7. purple
8. white
9. black

Down

1. green
2. yellow
3. pink
5. orange

Food Words

Say each word out loud. Write the English word next to it.

queso

_____

leche

_____

papa

_____

jugo

pan

_____

pollo

_____

ensalada

_____

Color the blocks with letters.
Do not color the blocks with numbers. What word did you find? _____

7	x	7	7	7	7	7	7	7	7	7	x	7	7	7	7	7	7	7
7	x	7	7	7	7	7	7	7	7	7	x	7	7	7	7	7	7	7
7	x	7	7	7	7	7	7	7	7	7	x	7	7	7	7	7	7	7
7	x	7	x	x	x	7	x	x	x	7	x	7	7	7	x	x	x	7
7	x	7	x	7	x	7	x	7	7	7	x	x	x	7	x	7	x	7
7	x	7	x	x	x	7	x	7	7	7	x	7	x	7	x	x	x	7
7	x	7	x	7	7	7	x	7	7	7	x	7	x	7	x	7	7	7
7	x	7	x	x	x	7	x	x	x	7	x	7	x	7	x	x	x	7

Food Riddles

Answer the riddles. Use the size and shape of the word blocks along with the answers at the bottom to help you.

I come from an animal. Kids like to eat my drumstick. What am I?

I can be full of holes. Mice like me. What am I?

I am squeezed from fruit. Apple is a popular flavor. What am I?

I come from a cow. I can be regular or chocolate. What am I?

You can eat me baked, fried, or mashed. What am I?

You can eat me plain or with dressing. What am I?

I rise while baking in an oven. What am I?

queso   leche

papa   ensalada   pan

pollo   jugo

Use the Clues

Use the clues and the Word Bank at the bottom of the page to find the answers. Do not use any answer more than once.

1. You would not eat either of these fruits until you peel them.

_____   _____

2. Both of these drinks have a flavor.

_____   _____

3. You could put either of these on a sandwich.

_____   _____

4. These can be baked before eating. They all begin with the letter "p."

_____   _____   _____

5. These two go together on a cold winter day.

_____   _____

6. You use this liquid to wash this fruit.

_____   _____

7. Which word didn't you use?

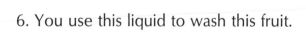

_____

queso	leche	papa	jugo	pan	pollo	ensalada
naranja	sopa	agua	sandwich	manzana	carne	plátano

A Square Meal

Refer to the Word Bank to write the name of each food in Spanish.

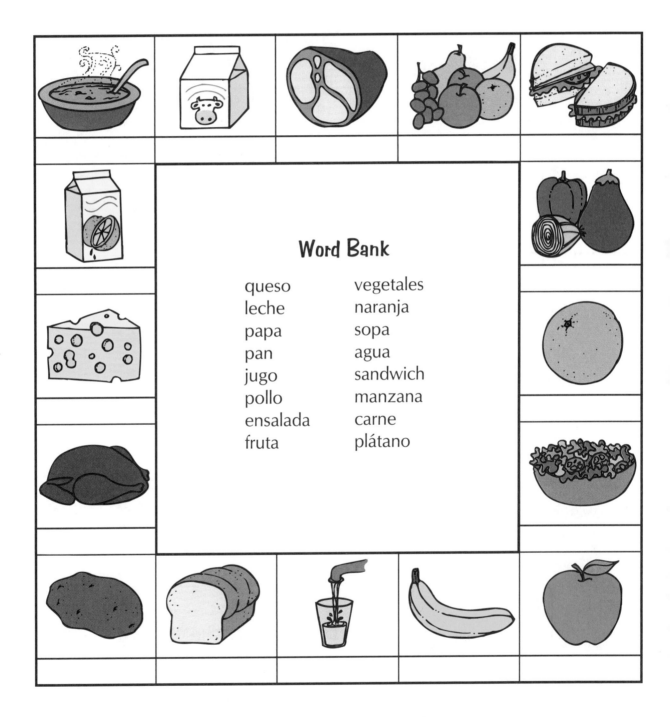

Word Bank

queso	vegetales
leche	naranja
papa	sopa
pan	agua
jugo	sandwich
pollo	manzana
ensalada	carne
fruta	plátano

Eat It Up

Write the Spanish for the clue words in the crossword puzzle.

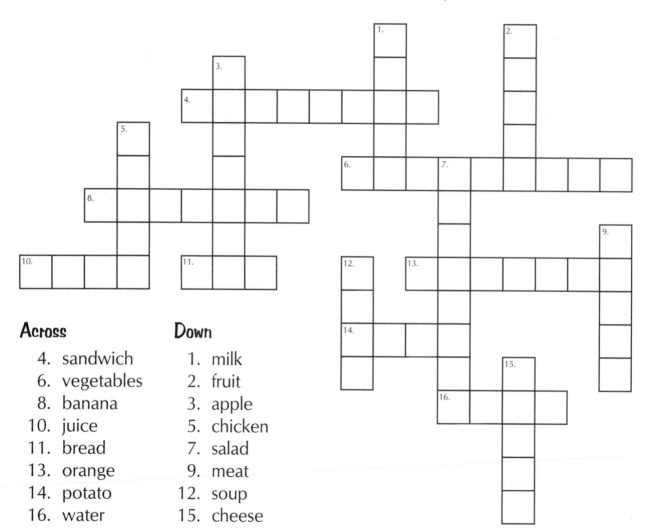

Across

4. sandwich
6. vegetables
8. banana
10. juice
11. bread
13. orange
14. potato
16. water

Down

1. milk
2. fruit
3. apple
5. chicken
7. salad
9. meat
12. soup
15. cheese

Word Bank			
ensalada	plátano	manzana	papa
pan	naranja	fruta	queso
carne	sopa	jugo	vegetales
sandwich	leche	agua	pollo

Use the Clues

Answer the questions. Use the clues and the Spanish words at the bottom of the page. You may use answers more than once.

1. Both words begin with the same letter, and both animals have feathers.

_____ _____

2. These two animals walk and are house pets.

_____ _____

3. Both animals begin with the same letter. One quacks and the other barks.

_____ _____

4. Both of these animals like to live in the water.

_____ _____

5. These animals do not have fur or feathers.

_____ _____

6. The first animal likes to chase and catch the second animal. They both end with the letter o.

_____ _____

| gato | perro | pájaro |
| pez | pato | culebra |

Three Little Kittens

Draw a picture to match the Spanish phrase in each box.

seis pájaros	cuatro perros
nueve abejas	siete osos
tres gatos	dos vacas
cinco patos	ocho caballos
diez ranas	un pez

Animal Match

Copy the Spanish word under each picture.

oso	rana	caballo	vaca

_____ _____ _____ _____

elefante	oveja	puerco	gallina

_____ _____ _____ _____

gato	tortuga	mariposa	dinosaurio

_____ _____ _____ _____

Write the Spanish for each animal name.

1. butterfly _____

2. sheep _____

3. cat _____

4. dinosaur _____

5. chicken _____

6. pig _____

7. cow _____

8. bear _____

9. elephant _____

10. horse _____

11. turtle _____

12. frog _____

   Spanish: Grade 3

Clothes to Color

Cut out pictures and glue them next to the correct words.

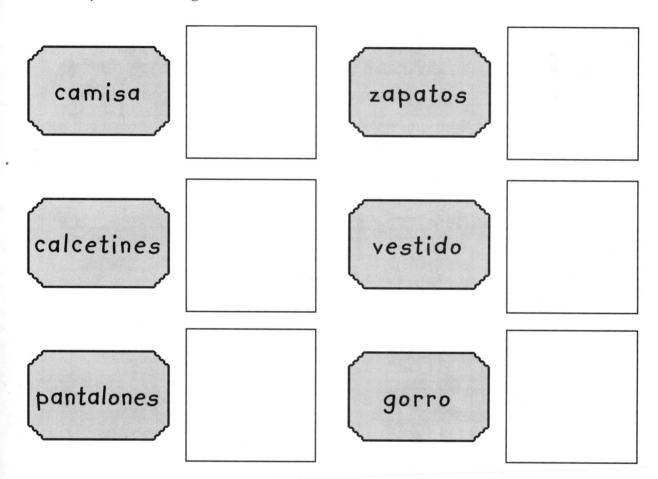

Try this: Color each block with a letter X inside. Do not color the blocks with numbers. What hidden word did you find? _____

8	8	8	8	8	8	8	8	8	8	8	8	8	8	8	8	8	8	8	8	8	8
8	8	x	x	x	8	x	x	x	8	x	x	x	8	x	x	x	8	x	x	x	8
8	8	x	8	x	8	x	8	x	8	x	8	x	8	x	8	x	8	x	8	x	8
8	8	x	x	x	8	x	8	x	8	x	8	8	8	x	8	8	8	x	8	x	8
8	8	8	8	x	8	x	x	x	8	x	8	8	8	x	8	8	8	x	x	x	8
8	8	x	8	x	8	8	8	8	8	8	8	8	8	x	8	8	8	8	8	8	8
8	8	x	x	x	8	8	8	8	8	8	8	8	8	8	8	8	8	8	8	8	8

Clothes Closet

Refer to the Word Bank and write the Spanish word for each item of clothing pictured.

Word Bank			
vestido	calcetines	botas	zapatos
sombrero	cinturón	falda	chaqueta
guantes	pantalones cortos	pantalones	camisa

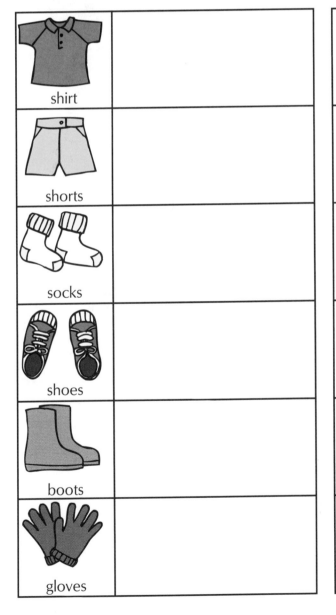

shirt		pants	
shorts		hat	
socks		skirt	
shoes		belt	
boots		dress	
gloves		jacket	

Name _____

Dressing Up

Write the Spanish word for each clue in the crossword puzzle.

Across

1. shoes
4. socks
7. dress
8. gloves
9. hat
10. shirt

Down

2. pants
3. skirt
4. jacket
5. belt
6. boots

Word Bank

cinturón	botas	camisa
guantes	calcetines	sombrero
chaqueta	falda	zapatos
pantalones	vestido	

Matching Clothes

At the bottom of each picture, write the English word that matches the Spanish and the pictures. Write the Spanish words next to the English at the bottom of the page.

falda 	zapatos 	pantalones cortos 	cinturón 
abrigo 	calcetines 	vestido 	botas 
guantes 	pantalones 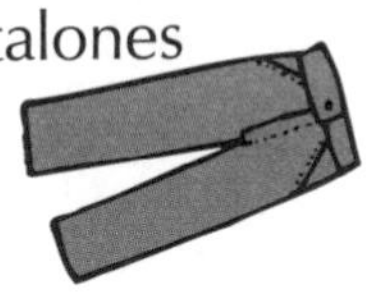	chaqueta 	blusa 
gorro 	sandalias 	camisa 	

1. skirt _____

2. belt _____

3. jacket _____

4. socks _____

5. coat _____

6. shirt _____

7. sandals _____

8. dress _____

9. cap _____

10. pants _____

11. gloves _____

12. boots _____

13. shoes _____

14. blouse _____

15. shorts _____

Spanish: Grade 3

Face Riddles

Can you guess the answers to the following riddles? Use the size and shape of the letter blocks to write the Spanish word. The answers at the bottom will help you.

There are two of me. Sometimes I need glasses. What am I?

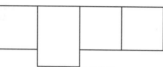

I like to be washed and combed. What am I?

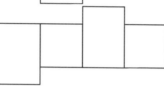

I help hold up glasses. When I feel an itch, I sneeze. What am I?

Everyone's looks a little different, in spite of the shape. What am I?

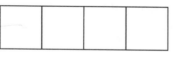

We grow, get loose, fall out, and grow again. What are we?

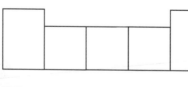

"Open wide" is often said when I am too small. What am I?

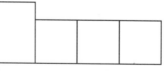

Does your mom always tell you to wash behind us? What are we?

nariz	pelo	dientes
ojos	orejas	cara	boca

A Blank Face

Fill in the blanks with the missing letters. Use the Spanish words below to help you.

Crossword puzzle answers:
- Across/Down: dientes, pelo, orejas, boca, nariz, ojos

Word bank: ~~nariz~~   ~~pelo~~   ~~dientes~~   ~~ojos~~   ~~orejas~~   cara   ~~boca~~

Which word didn't you use? _____

Color each block that has a letter k inside. Do not color the blocks with numbers. What hidden word did you find? _____

k	5	5	5	5	5	5	5	5	5	5	5	5	5	5	5
k	5	5	5	5	5	5	5	5	5	5	5	5	5	5	5
k	5	5	5	5	5	5	5	5	5	5	5	5	5	5	5
k	k	k	5	k	k	k	5	k	k	k	5	k	k	k	5
k	5	k	5	k	5	k	5	k	5	5	5	k	5	k	5
k	5	k	5	k	5	k	5	k	5	5	5	k	5	k	5
k	k	k	5	k	k	k	5	k	k	k	5	k	k	k	k

How Are You?

Label each facial feature with a Spanish word from the Word Bank.

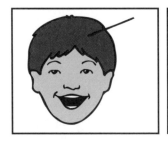  

_____ _____ _____

  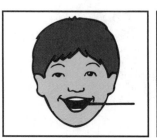 

_____ _____ _____ _____

Copy the Spanish word that matches each face pictured.

 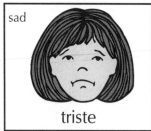 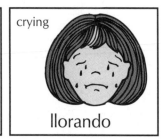

happy — alegre   sad — triste   crying — llorando

_____ _____ _____

smiling — sonriendo   angry — enojado   thinking — pensando

_____ _____ _____

Happy Faces

Write the Spanish for the clue words in the crossword puzzle.

Across

1. sad
3. nose
5. eyes
6. thinking
8. face
11. smiling
13. crying

Down

2. angry
4. happy
7. teeth
9. ears
10. mouth
12. hair

Word Bank

llorando	orejas	sonriendo	ojos
pelo	nariz	triste	cara
dientes	alegre	enojado	boca
pensando			

Matching Family

Cut out a picture of a family out of a magazine. Glue each picture next to the correct word.

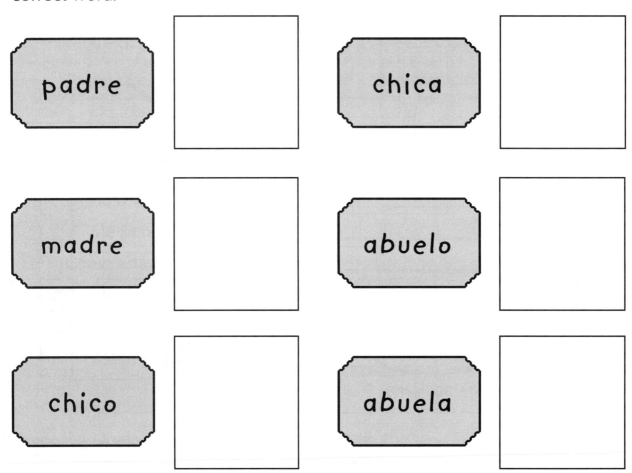

padre

madre

chico

chica

abuelo

abuela

Try this: Color each block with a letter inside. Do not color the blocks with numbers. What hidden word did you find? _____

2	2	2	2	2	2	2	2	2	2	2	2	2	m	2	2	2	2	2	2	2	2
2	2	2	2	2	2	2	2	2	2	2	2	2	m	2	2	2	2	2	2	2	2
m	m	m	m	m	2	m	m	m	2	2	m	m	m	2	m	m	m	2	m	m	m
m	2	m	2	m	2	m	2	m	2	2	m	2	m	2	m	2	m	2	m	2	m
m	2	m	2	m	2	m	2	m	2	2	m	2	m	2	m	2	2	2	m	m	m
m	2	m	2	m	2	m	2	m	2	2	m	2	m	2	m	2	2	2	m	2	2
m	2	m	2	m	2	m	m	m	m	m	2	m	m	m	2	m	2	2	2	m	m	m

Family Ties

In each box, copy the Spanish word for family members.

la familia		el hermano	
	family		brother
el padre		la hermana	
	father		sister
la madre		el tío	
	mother		uncle
el hijo		la tía	
	son		aunt
la hija		el abuelo	
	daughter		grandfather
los primos		la abuela	
	cousins		grandmother

Write the Spanish words from above next to the English words.

sister _____   family _____   father _____

grandfather _____   cousins _____   mother _____

grandmother _____   brother _____   daughter _____

uncle _____   aunt _____   son _____

My Family

Write the Spanish word for each clue in the crossword puzzle.

Across

2. son
3. aunt
5. sister
7. grandmother
8. brother
10. cousins

Down

1. mother
2. daughter
4. family
6. grandfather
9. uncle
10. father

Word Bank

familia	hermano	hijo	tía
primos	madre	tío	abuelo
padre	hermana	hija	abuela

Name ______________________________

Family Tree

Refer to the Word Bank to write the Spanish word that matches each picture.

Word Bank

el hermano
el tío
la abuela
la hija
los primos
el hijo
la hermana
el abuelo
la madre
el padre
la familia
la tía

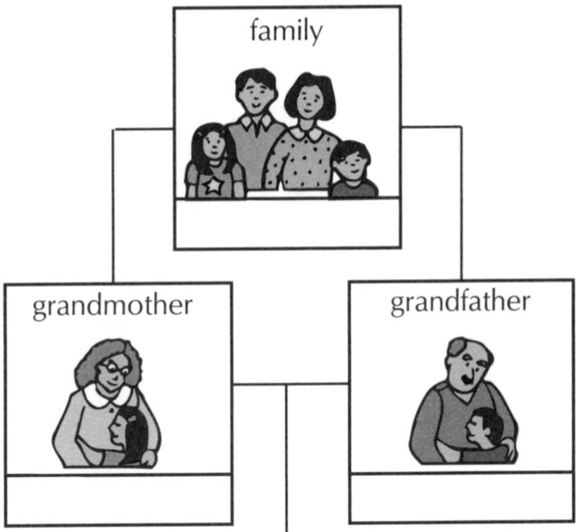

family
grandmother
grandfather

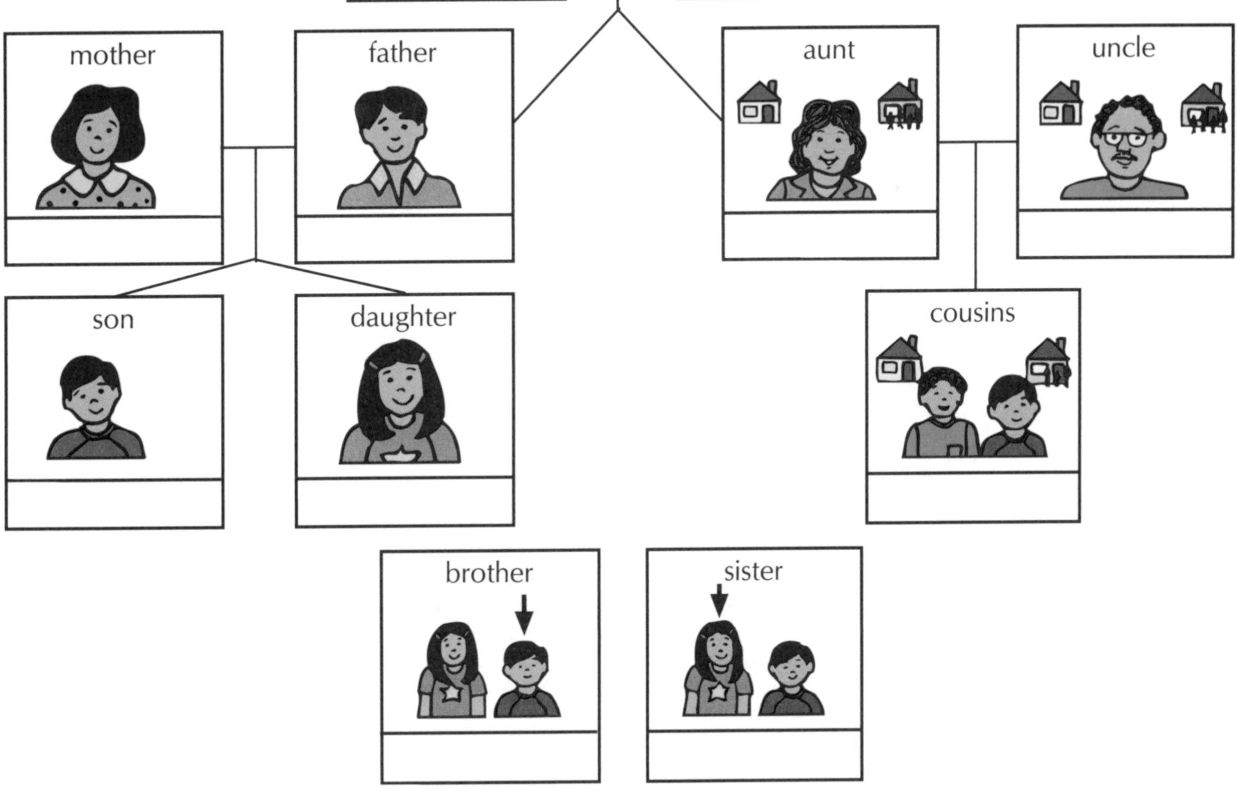

mother
father
aunt
uncle
son
daughter
cousins
brother
sister

Places, Please

Cut out pictures that match the words below. Glue each picture next to the correct word.

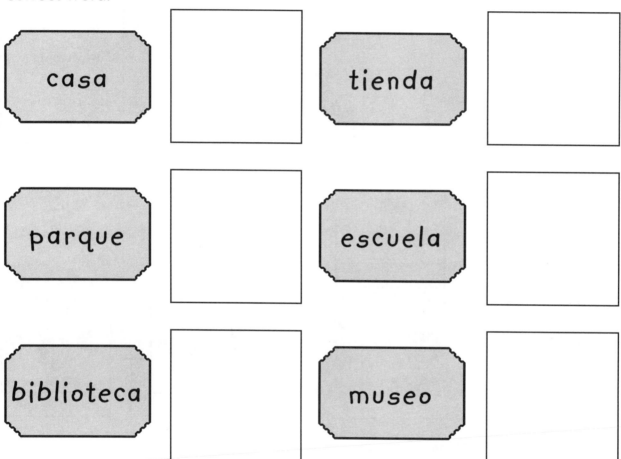

casa

tienda

parque

escuela

biblioteca

museo

Try this: Color each block with a letter Y inside. Do not color the blocks with numbers. What hidden word did you find? _____

9	9	9	9	9	9	9	9	9	9	9	9	9	9	9	9	9
y	y	y	9	y	y	y	9	9	y	y	y	9	y	y	y	9
y	9	y	9	y	9	y	9	9	y	9	9	9	y	9	y	9
y	9	9	9	y	9	y	9	9	y	y	y	9	y	9	y	9
y	9	y	9	y	9	y	9	9	9	9	y	9	y	9	y	9
y	y	y	9	y	y	y	y	9	y	y	y	9	y	y	y	y
9	9	9	9	9	9	9	9	9	9	9	9	9	9	9	9	9

Name _____

A Place for Riddles

Answer the riddles. Use the size and shape of the letter blocks to write the Spanish words. The answers at the bottom of the page will help you.

People live in me. What am I?

If you want to buy something, you come to me. What am I?

People like to come to me for playing and relaxing. What am I?

I am filled with books that you can borrow. What am I?

I am filled with children, desks, and books. What am I?

I often have dinosaur bones. What am I?

escuela   museo   casa
biblioteca   tienda   parque

© Carson-Dellosa

53

Spanish: Grade 3

Where Am I?

Refer to the Word Bank and write the Spanish for each place in the community pictured.

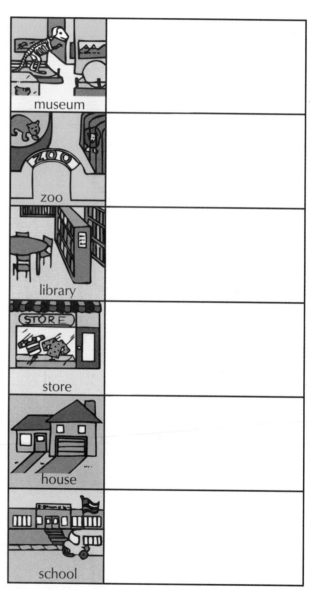

Word Bank	
escuela	granja	biblioteca	tienda
museo	casa	apartamento	zoológico
iglesia	restaurante	cine	parque

Fitting In

Write the Spanish words from the Word Bank in these word blocks. Write the English meanings below the blocks.

1.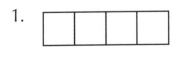

_____

2.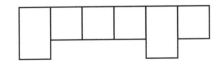

_____

3.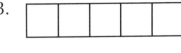

_____

4.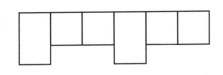

_____

5.

_____

6.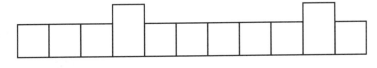

_____

7.

_____

8.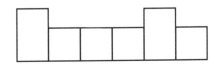

_____

9.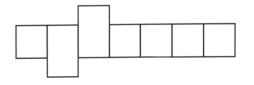

_____

10.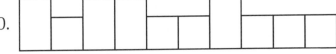

_____

Around the House

Copy the Spanish words. Then, write the English words below them.

casa		sofá	
_____		_____	
_____		_____	
cocina		cama	
_____		_____	
_____		_____	
sala		lámpara	
_____		_____	
_____		_____	
dormitorio		cuchara	
_____		_____	
_____		_____	

Word Bank

couch	kitchen	lamp	spoon
bedroom	bed	house	living room

Around the Block

Write the Spanish words from the Word Bank that fit in these word blocks.
Write the English below the blocks.

Word Bank

casa	dormitorio	lámpara
cocina	sofá	cuchara
sala	cama	

1.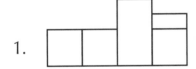

2.

3.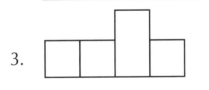

4.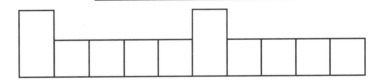

5.

6.

7.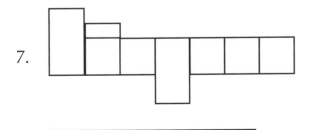

8.

Around the House

Write the Spanish words for the clue words in the crossword puzzle.

Across

2. kitchen
3. lamp
5. towel
8. living room
9. telephone
11. stove

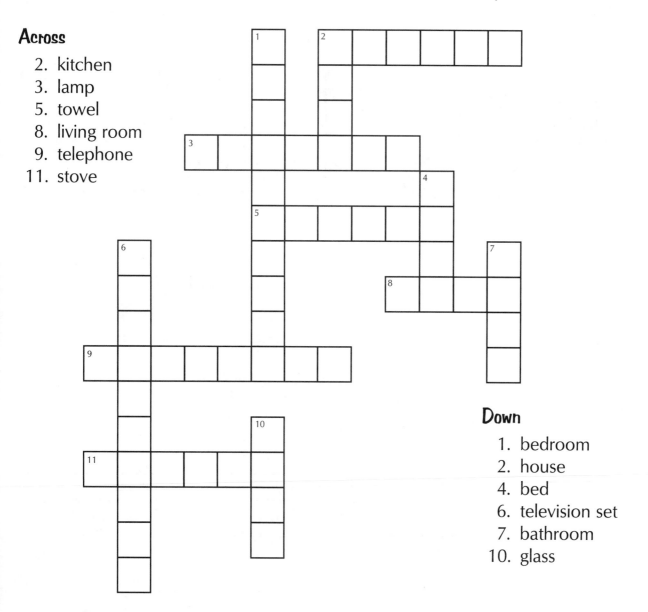

Down

1. bedroom
2. house
4. bed
6. television set
7. bathroom
10. glass

Word Bank

baño	cocina	lámpara	televisión
dormitorio	teléfono	toalla	cama
vaso	casa	estufa	sala

Match Words and Pictures

Cut out pictures from a magazine and glue each picture next to the correct word.

silla

borrador

mesa

lápiz

tijeras

libro

Use the Clues

Use the clues and the words at the bottom of the page. Do not use any answer more than once.

1. Both words begin with the letter *p*. You write <u>with</u> one and write <u>on</u> one. What are they?

_____   _____

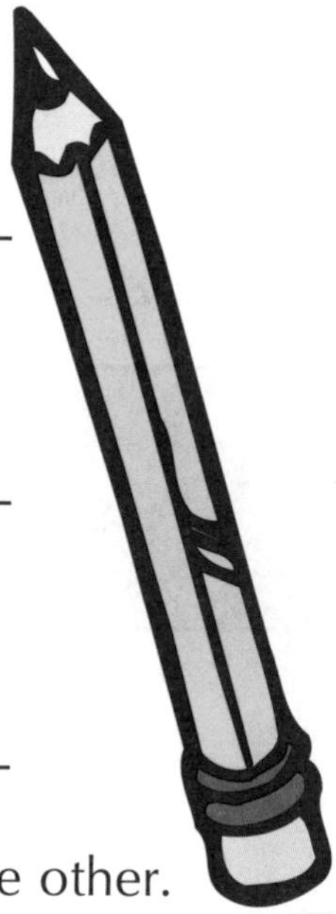

2. You can sit at either one of these when you need to write.

_____   _____

3. You could exit through either one of these in case of fire.

_____   _____

4. Both words end with the letter *o*. They both have pages.

_____   _____

5. These two words go together because one is on the end of the other.

_____   _____

6. Both words have an *i* as their second letter. One is used for cutting and the other is used for sitting.

_____   _____

silla	mesa	tijeras	libro	borrador	ventana
puerta	lápiz	cuaderno	papel	escritorio	pluma

Around the Room

In each box, copy the Spanish word for the classroom object pictured.

silla		mesa	
puerta		pluma	
ventana		borrador	
lápiz		cuaderno	
papel		libro	
escritorio		tijeras	

Write the Spanish words from above next to the English words.

window _____   chair _____   table _____

eraser _____   scissors _____   door _____

desk _____   pen _____   notebook _____

paper _____   book _____   pencil _____

         Spanish: Grade 3

A Fitting Design

Write the Spanish words from the Word Bank that fit in these word blocks. Write the English meanings below the blocks.

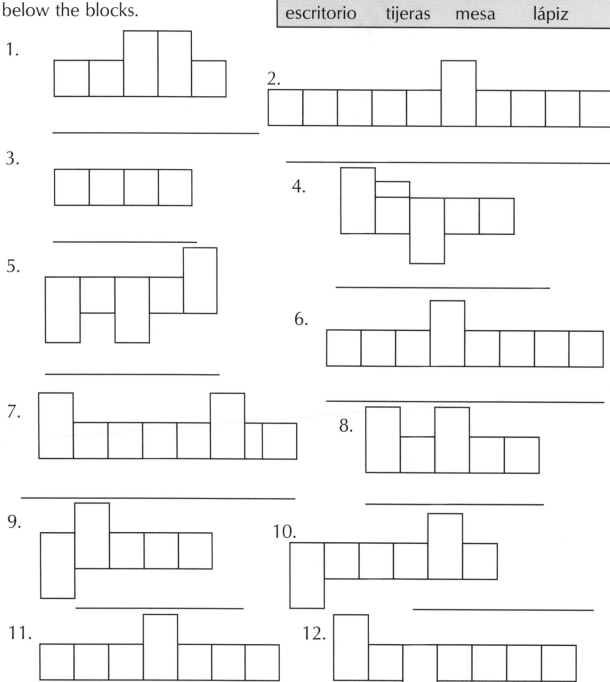

1.

2.

3.

4.

5.

6.

7.

8.

9.

10.

11.

12.

Classroom Clutter

Draw a picture to illustrate each of the Spanish words. Refer to the Word Bank at the bottom of the page to help you.

silla	ventana
mesa	puerta
tijeras	papel
libro	cuaderno
lápiz	escritorio
borrador	pluma

Word Bank

eraser	door	scissors	pen	window	paper
chair	notebook	pencil	desk	book	table

Show and Tell

Write the Spanish for each clue in the crossword puzzle.

Across

1. notebook
5. scissors
7. pen
8. eraser
10. pencil
11. table
12. chair

Down

2. desk
3. window
4. book
6. door
9. paper

Word Bank

escritorio	mesa	libro	silla	tijeras	puerta
lápiz	ventana	borrador	cuaderno	papel	pluma

Songs and Chants

Food Song
(to the tune of "She'll Be Coming 'Round the Mountain")

Queso is cheese, yum, yum, yum. (clap, clap)
Leche is milk, yum, yum, yum. (clap, clap)
Papa is potato.
Jugo is juice.
Pan is bread, yum, yum, yum! (clap, clap)

Pollo is chicken, yum, yum, yum. (clap, clap)
Ensalada is salad, yum, yum, yum. (clap, clap)
Queso, leche, papa,
jugo, pan, pollo, ensalada,
yum, yum, yum, yum, yum! (clap, clap)

Community Song
(to the tune of "Here We Go 'Round the Mulberry Bush")

Escuela is school,
casa is house,
biblioteca is library;

museo museum;
tienda is store;
parque is the park for me!

Songs

¡Hola, chicos!
(to the tune of "Goodnight Ladies")

¡Hola, chico! ¡Hola, chica!
¡Hola, chicos! ¿Cómo están hoy?
¡Hola, chico! ¡Hola, chica!
¡Hola, chicos! ¿Cómo están hoy?

Los días de la semana
(to the tune of "Clementine")

Domingo, lunes,
martes, miércoles,
jueves, viernes, sábado,
domingo, lunes,
martes, miércoles,
jueves, viernes, sábado. (Repitan)

Learning Cards

Cut out the learning cards. Practice saying the Spanish words using the learning cards.

levántense	**cierren**
siéntense	**cállensen**
abran	**póngansen**

Learning Cards

close	**stand up**
be quiet	**sit down**
line up	**open**

Name _____

Learning Cards

Cut out the learning cards. Practice saying the Spanish words using the learning cards.

párense	**pinten**
corten	**dibujen**
peguen	**canten**

Learning Cards

paint	stop
draw	cut
sing	paste

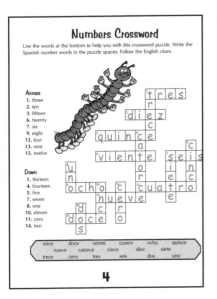

Numbers Crossword

Use the words at the bottom to help you with this crossword puzzle. Write the
Spanish number words in the puzzle spaces. Follow the English clues.

Across
1. three
2. ten
3. fifteen
6. twenty
7. six
9. eight
12. four
13. nine
15. twelve

Down
1. thirteen
4. fourteen
5. five
7. seven
8. one
10. eleven
11. zero
14. two

Crossword answers: tres, diez, quince, viente, seis, ocho, nueve, cuatro, doce, un

Word list: once, doce, veinte, cuatro, ocho, quince, nueve, catorce, cinco, diez, siete, trece, cero, tres, seis, dos, uno

4

Numbers

After each numeral, write the number word in Spanish. Refer to the words below to
help you.

Word Bank					
veinte	cuatro	nueve	diez	dieciseite	quince
doce	once	trece	siete	uno	tres
catorce	dos	cero	ocho	cinco	dieciséis
diecinueve		dieciocho		seis	

0 cero
1 uno
2 dos
3 tres
4 cuatro
5 cinco
6 seis
7 siete
8 ocho
9 nueve
10 diez

11 once
12 dos
13 trece
14 catorce
15 quince
16 dieciséis
17 diecisiete
18 dieciocho
19 diecinueve
20 veinte

5

Numbers Illustration

Write the number. Draw that many things in the box. The first one is done for you.

★★★★ ★★★★		
ocho means 8	cinco means 5	diecisiete means 17
doce means 12	uno means 1	dos means 2
catorce means 14	nueve means 9	veinte means 20
siete means 7	cuatro means 4	quince means 15

Pictures Will Vary.

6

Who Is It?

Write the names of people you may know that fit each description below.

tú–informal or familiar form of you	
someone you refer to by first name	
your sister or brother (or cousin)	
a classmate	*Answers Will Vary.*
a close friend	
a child younger than yourself	

usted–formal or polite form of you	
someone with a title	
an older person	
a stranger	*Answers Will Vary.*
a person of authority	

How would you speak to each person below? Write *tú* or *usted* after each person
named.

1. Dr. Hackett usted
2. Susana tú
3. a four-year-old tú
4. your grandfather usted
5. the governor usted
6. your best friend tú
7. your sister tú
8. the principal usted
9. a classmate tú
10. a stranger usted

7

Masculine and Feminine

All Spanish nouns and adjectives have gender. This means they are either masculine
or feminine. Here are two basic rules to help determine the gender of words. There
are other rules for gender which you will learn as you study more Spanish.

1. Spanish words ending in -o are usually masculine.
2. Spanish words ending in -a are usually feminine.

Write the following words in the charts to determine their gender. Write the English
meanings to the right. Use a Spanish-English dictionary if you need help.

maestra, libro, escritorio, negro, abrigo, sopa, tienda,
amigo, ventana, pluma, maestro, vestido, fruta, museo,
silla, puerta, anaranjado, amiga, camisa, queso, casa,
rojo, cuaderno, blanco, falda, chaqueta

Masculine		Feminine	
words ending in -o	meaning of the word	words ending in -a	meaning of the word
amigo	friend (male)	maestra	teacher (female)
rojo	red	silla	chair
libro	book	ventana	window
cuaderno	notebook	puerta	door
escriturio	desk	pluma	pen
anaranjado	orange	amiga	friend (female)
museo	museum	falda	skirt
blanco	white	camisa	shirt
negro	black	chaqueta	jacket
maestro	teacher (male)	sopa	soup
abrigo	coat	fruta	fruit
vestido	dress	tienda	store
queso	cheese	casa	house

8

It's a Small World

In Spanish, there are four ways to say "the"—*el, la, los,* and *las.* The definite article (the)
agrees with its noun in gender (masculine or feminine) and number (singular or plural).

Masculine singular nouns go with *el.* Feminine singular nouns go with *la.*

Examples: *el libro* (the book)   *el papel* (the paper)
la silla (the chair)   *la regla* (the ruler)

Masculine plural nouns go with *los.* Feminine plural nouns go with *las.*

Examples: *los libros* (the books)   *los papeles* (the papers)
las sillas (the chairs)   *las reglas* (the rulers)

Refer to the Word Bank to complete the chart. Write the singular and plural forms and
the correct definite articles. The first ones have been done for you.

Word Bank				
cuaderno	mesa	pluma	oso	falda
papel	gato	bota	silla	libro

English	Masculine Singular	Masculine Plural
the book	el libro	los libros
the paper	el papel	los papeles
the notebook	el cuaderno	los cuadernos
the cat	el gato	los gatos
the bear	el oso	los osos

English	Feminine Singular	Feminine Plural
the chair	la silla	las sillas
the table	la mesa	las mesas
the boot	la bota	las botas
the skirt	la falda	las faldas
the pen	la pluma	las plumas

9

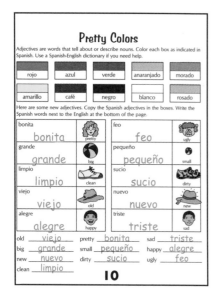

Pretty Colors

Adjectives are words that tell about or describe nouns. Color each box as indicated in Spanish. Use a Spanish-English dictionary if you need help.

rojo	azul	verde	anaranjado	morado

amarillo	café	negro	blanco	rosado

Here are some new adjectives. Copy the Spanish adjectives in the boxes. Write the Spanish words next to the English at the bottom of the page.

bonita	bonita	(pretty)	feo	feo	(ugly)
grande	grande	(big)	pequeño	pequeño	(small)
limpio	limpio	(clean)	sucio	sucio	(dirty)
viejo	viejo	(old)	nuevo	nuevo	(new)
alegre	alegre	(happy)	triste	triste	(sad)

old __viejo__ pretty __bonita__ sad __triste__
big __grande__ small __pequeño__ happy __alegre__
new __nuevo__ dirty __sucio__ ugly __feo__
clean __limpio__

10

Words to Describe

Descriptive adjectives are words that describe nouns. Refer to the Word Bank to write the Spanish adjective that describes each picture.

Word Bank

alegre	grande	nuevo	pequeño	feo	rico
limpio	sucio	bonita	triste	viejo	pobre
alto	bajo	abierto	cerrado		

| large | new | ugly | happy |
| grande | nuevo | feo | alegre |

| old | sad | small | clean |
| viejo | triste | pequeño | limpio |

| pretty | dirty | tall | open |
| bonita | sucio | alto | abierto |

| rich | short | closed | poor |
| rico | bajo | cerrado | pobre |

11

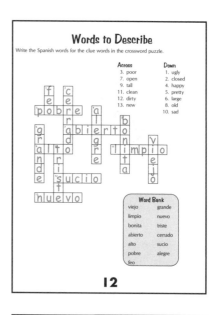

Words to Describe

Write the Spanish words for the clue words in the crossword puzzle.

Across
3. poor
7. open
9. tall
11. clean
12. dirty
13. new

Down
1. ugly
2. closed
4. happy
5. pretty
6. large
8. old
10. sad

(crossword puzzle filled in with: feo, cerrado, pobre, alto, abierto, bonita, grande, alegre, limpio, viejo, sucio, huevo)

Word Bank

viejo	grande
limpio	nuevo
bonita	triste
abierto	cerrado
alto	sucio
pobre	alegre
feo	

12

Action Words

In each box, copy the Spanish action verbs. Then, write the English word below it.

comer	hablar
comer	hablar
to eat	to speak
beber	limpiar
beber	limpiar
to drink	to clean
dormir	mirar
dormir	mirar
to sleep	to look at
tocar	dar
tocar	dar
to touch	to give

Word Bank

| to touch | to look at | to eat | to give |
| to drink | to speak | to clean | to sleep |

13

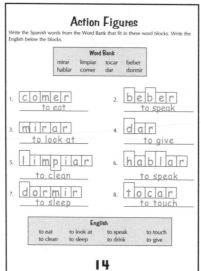

Action Figures

Write the Spanish words from the Word Bank that fit in these word blocks. Write English below the blocks.

Word Bank

| mirar | limpiar | tocar | beber |
| hablar | comer | dar | dormir |

1. c o m e r
   to eat

2. b e b e r
   to speak

3. m i r a r
   to look at

4. d a r
   to give

5. l i m p i a r
   to clean

6. h a b l a r
   to speak

7. d o r m i r
   to sleep

8. t o c a r
   to touch

English

| to eat | to look at | to speak | to touch |
| to clean | to sleep | to drink | to give |

14

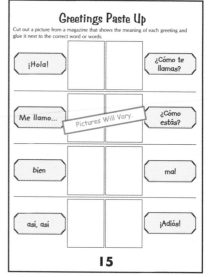

Greetings Paste Up

Cut out a picture from a magazine that shows the meaning of each greeting and glue it next to the correct word or words.

¡Hola!			¿Cómo te llamas?
Me llamo...	Pictures Will Vary.		¿Cómo estás?
bien			mal
así, así			¡Adiós!

15

What's Your Name?

Word Bank

I'm so-so.	What's your name?	I'm well/fine.
I'm ___ years old.	I'm not doing well.	My name is ___.
I'm so-so.	How are you?	How old are you?

Refer to the Word Bank to translate the Spanish questions and answers into English.

1. ¿Cómo te llamas? _What is your name?_
   Me llamo _My name is_ .
2. ¿Cómo estás? _How are you?_
   Estoy bien/mal/así así. _I'm fine. I'm not well. I'm so-so._
3. ¿Cuántos años tienes? _How old are you?_
   Tengo ___ años. _I am ___ years old._

Word Bank

hello	please	friend	yes
no	thank you	goodbye	See you later!

Write the English meaning after the Spanish word.

4. hola _hello_
5. amigo, amiga _friend (m/f)_
6. sí _yes_
7. no _no_
8. por favor _please_
9. gracias _thank you_
10. ¡Hasta luego! _See you later!_
11. adiós _goodbye_

16

Word Blocks

Write the Spanish words from the Word Bank that fit in these word blocks. Don't forget the punctuation. Write the English meanings below the blocks.

1. h o l a — hello
2. p o r   f a v o r — please
3. n o — no
4. ¡ H a s t a   l u e g o ! — See you later!
5. ¿ C ó m o   e s t á s ? — How are you?
6. ¿ C ó m o   t e   l l a m a s ? — What is your name?
7. a d i ó s — goodbye
8. E s t o y   b i e n . — I am fine.

Spanish Word Bank

por favor	adiós	Estoy bien.
hola	¡Hasta luego!	¿Cómo te llamas?
no	¿Cómo estás?	

17

Greetings

Write the English meaning of the Spanish words and phrases.

1. señor _Mr._
2. señora _Mrs._
3. señorita _Miss_
4. maestro _teacher (male)_
5. maestra _teacher (female)_
6. ¡Buenos días! _Good morning!_
7. ¡Buenas tardes! _Good afternoon!_
8. ¡Buenas noches! _Good night!_
9. Vamos a contar. _Let's count_

Word Bank

Mr.	Good night!	Good morning!
Good afternoon!	teacher (female)	teacher (male)
Miss	Let's count.	Mrs.

Draw a picture to show the time of day that you use each expression.

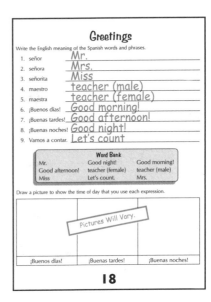

Pictures Will Vary.

¡Buenos días!	¡Buenas tardes!	¡Buenas noches!

18

Spanish Greetings

Write the Spanish word for each clue in the crossword puzzle.

Across
1. bad
4. good
7. teacher (male)
9. friend (female)
10. Mr.
11. Miss

Down
2. friend (male)
3. hello
5. thank you
6. goodbye
7. teacher (female)
8. Mrs.

Word Bank

amiga	mal
señora	señor
maestra	bien
adiós	hola
señorita	gracias
amigo	maestro

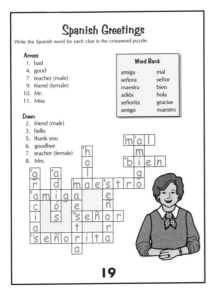

19

Yesterday and Today

Write the Spanish words for the days of the week. Remember, in Spanish-speaking countries, Monday is the first day of the week.

Word Bank

miércoles	jueves	sábado
viernes	lunes	martes
	domingo	

Monday	lunes
Tuesday	martes
Wednesday	miércoles
Thursday	jueves
Friday	viernes
Saturday	sábado
Sunday	domingo

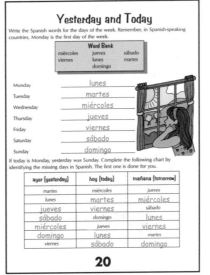

If today is Monday, yesterday was Sunday. Complete the following chart by identifying the missing days in Spanish. The first one is done for you.

ayer (yesterday)	hoy (today)	mañana (tomorrow)
martes	miércoles	jueves
lunes	martes	miércoles
jueves	viernes	sábado
sábado	domingo	lunes
miércoles	jueves	viernes
domingo	lunes	martes
viernes	sábado	domingo

20

Rain in April

Refer to the Word Bank to write the Spanish word for the given month. Then, in the box, draw a picture of something that happens in that month of the year. Remember that Spanish months do not begin with capital letters.

Word Bank

agosto	septiembre	noviembre	mayo
junio	enero	octubre	febrero
marzo	julio	diciembre	abril

January		July	
enero	Pictures Will Vary.	julio	Pictures Will Vary.
February		August	
febrero		agosto	
March		September	
marzo		septiembre	
April		October	
abril		octubre	
May		November	
mayo		noviembre	
June		December	
junio		diciembre	

21

Writing Practice

Copy the following paragraph in your best handwriting. Practice reading it out loud.

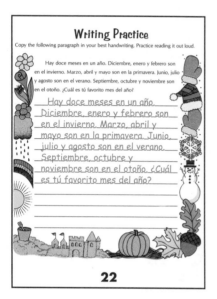

Hay doce meses en un año. Diciembre, enero y febrero son en el invierno. Marzo, abril y mayo son en la primavera. Junio, julio y agosto son en el verano. Septiembre, octubre y noviembre son en el otoño. ¿Cuál es tú favorito mes del año?

Hay doce meses en un año. Diciembre, enero y febrero son en el invierno. Marzo, abril y mayo son en la primavera. Junio, julio y agosto son en el verano. Septiembre, octubre y noviembre son en el otoño. ¿Cuál es tú favorito mes del año?

22

Birds of Color

Color the birds according to the words listed.

23

House of Colors

Color each crayon with the correct color for the Spanish word. Add something with your favorite color.

Pictures Will Vary.

■ rojo   ■ negro   □ café   ▨ rosado
■ azul   □ amarillo   □ blanco   ■ verde

24

Color the Flowers

Color each flower with the correct color for the Spanish word.

■ azul   ■ café   □ amarillo   ■ rosado
■ verde   ■ rojo   ■ morado   □ anaranjado

25

Moving Colors

Color the pictures according to the words listed.

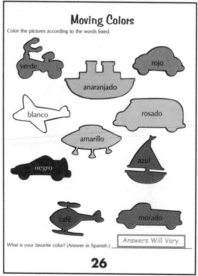

What is your favorite color? (Answer in Spanish.)   Answers Will Vary.

26

Color Crossword

Write the correct Spanish color words in the spaces. Follow the English color clues.

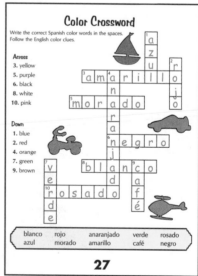

Across
3. yellow
5. purple
6. black
8. white
10. pink

Down
1. blue
2. red
4. orange
7. green
9. brown

| blanco | rojo | anaranjado | verde | rosado |
| azul | morado | amarillo | café | negro |

27

Colorful Flowers

Color the flowers according to the Spanish color words shown.

28

Draw and Color

In each box, write the Spanish color word. Use the Word Bank below to help you.
Then, draw and color a picture of something that is usually that color.

	Pictures Will Vary.	
red is rojo	orange is anaranjado	brown is café
blue is azul	purple is morado	black is negro
green is verde	yellow is amarillo	pink is rosado

Which Spanish color from the Word Bank is not used above? blanco

Word Bank

blanco	rojo	amarillo	rosado
azul	morado	verde	negro
	anaranjado	café	

29

Butterfly Garden

Color the butterfly garden as indicated in Spanish.

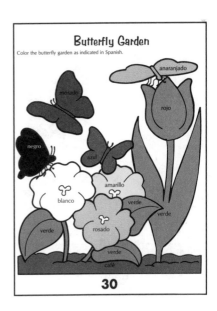

30

Across the Spectrum

Write the Spanish for each clue word in the crossword puzzle.

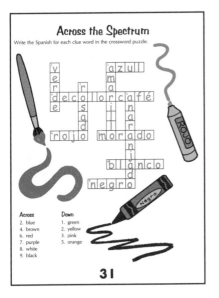

Across	Down
2. blue	1. green
4. brown	2. yellow
6. red	3. pink
7. purple	5. orange
8. white	
9. black	

31

Food Words

Say each word out loud. Write the English word next to it.

queso — cheese
leche — milk
papa — potato
jugo — juice
pan — bread
pollo — chicken
ensalada — salad

Color the blocks with letters.
Do not color the blocks with numbers. What word did you find? leche

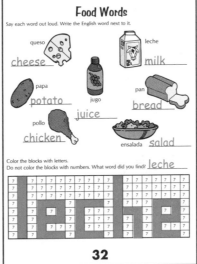

32

Food Riddles

Answer the riddles. Use the size and shape of the word blocks along with the answers at the bottom to help you.

I come from an animal. Kids like to eat my drumstick. What am I?	p o l l o
I can be full of holes. Mice like me. What am I?	q u e s o
I am squeezed from fruit. Apple is a popular flavor. What am I?	j u g o
I come from a cow. I can be regular or chocolate. What am I?	l e c h e
You can eat me baked, fried, or mashed. What am I?	p a p a
You can eat me plain or with dressing. What am I?	e n s a l a d a
I rise while baking in an oven. What am I?	p a n

queso	leche
papa	ensalada	pan
pollo	jugo

33

Use the Clues

Use the clues and the Word Bank at the bottom of the page to find the answers. Do not use any answer more than once.

1. You would not eat either of these fruits until you peel them.
naranja   plátano

2. Both of these drinks have a flavor.
leche   jugo

3. You could put either of these on a sandwich.
queso   carne

4. These can be baked before eating. They all begin with the letter "p."
papa   pan   pollo

5. These two go together on a cold winter day.
sopa   sandwich

6. You use this liquid to wash this fruit.
agua   manzana

7. Which word didn't you use?
ensalada

| queso | leche | papa | jugo | pan | pollo | ensalada |
| naranja | sopa | agua | sandwich | manzana | carne | plátano |

Check off each word as you use it.

34

A Square Meal

Refer to the Word Bank to write the name of each food in Spanish.

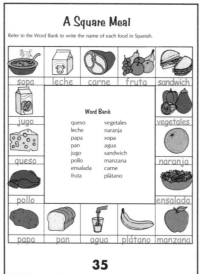

sopa	leche	carne	fruta	sandwich
jugo				vegetales
queso				naranja
pollo				ensalada
papa	pan	agua	plátano	manzana

Word Bank

queso	vegetales
leche	naranja
papa	sopa
pan	agua
jugo	sandwich
pollo	manzana
ensalada	carne
fruta	plátano

35

Eat It Up

Write the Spanish for the clue words in the crossword puzzle.

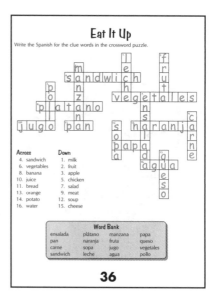

Across
4. sandwich
6. vegetables
8. banana
10. juice
11. bread
13. orange
14. potato
16. water

Down
1. milk
2. fruit
3. apple
5. chicken
7. salad
9. meat
12. soup
15. cheese

Word Bank

ensalada	plátano	manzana	papa
pan	naranja	fruta	queso
carne	sopa	jugo	vegetales
sandwich	leche	agua	pollo

36

Use the Clues

Answer the questions. Use the clues and the Spanish words at the bottom of the page. You may use answers more than once.

1. Both words begin with the same letter, and both animals have feathers.
pájaro   pato

2. These two animals walk and are house pets.
gato   perro

3. Both animals begin with the same letter. One quacks and the other barks.
perro   pato

4. Both of these animals like to live in the water.
pato   pez

5. These animals do not have fur or feathers.
culebra   pez

6. The first animal likes to chase and catch the second animal. They both end with the letter o.
gato   pájaro
(or perro/gato)

| gato | perro | pájaro |
| pez | pato | culebra |

37

Three Little Kittens

Draw a picture to match the Spanish phrase in each box.

seis pájaros	cuatro perros
nueve abejas	siete osos
tres gatos	dos vacas
cinco patos	ocho caballos
diez ranas	un pez

38

Animal Match

Copy the Spanish word under each picture.

oso	rana	caballo	vaca
oso	rana	caballo	vaca
elefante	oveja	puerco	gallina
elefante	oveja	puerco	gallina
gato	tortuga	mariposa	dinosaurio
gato	tortuga	mariposa	dinosaurio

Write the Spanish for each animal name.

1. butterfly   mariposa
2. sheep   oveja
3. cat   gato
4. dinosaur   dinosaurio
5. chicken   gallina
6. pig   puerco
7. cow   vaca
8. bear   oso
9. elephant   elefante
10. horse   caballo
11. turtle   tortuga
12. frog   rana

39

Spanish: Grade 3

76

© Carson-Dellosa

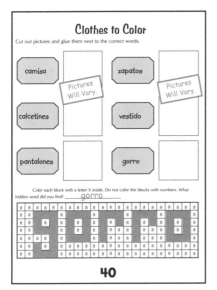

Clothes to Color

Cut out pictures and glue them next to the correct words.

camisa	Pictures Will Vary.
calcetines	vestido
pantalones	gorro

zapatos	Pictures Will Vary.

Color each block with a letter X inside. Do not color the blocks with numbers. What hidden word did you find? __gorro__

40

Clothes Closet

Refer to the Word Bank and write the Spanish word for each item of clothing pictured.

Word Bank

vestido	calcetines	botas	zapatos
sombrero	cinturón	falda	chaqueta
guantes	pantalones cortos	pantalones	camisa

shirt	camisa	pants	pantalones
shorts	pantalones cortos	hat	sombrero
socks	calcetines	skirt	falda
shoes	zapatos	belt	cinturón
boots	botas	dress	vestido
gloves	guantes	jacket	chaqueta

41

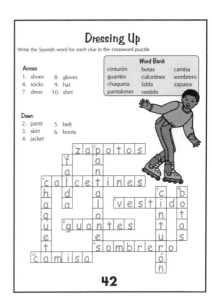

Dressing Up

Write the Spanish word for each clue in the crossword puzzle.

Across
1. shoes
4. socks
7. dress
8. gloves
9. hat
10. shirt

Down
2. pants
3. skirt
4. jacket
5. belt
6. boots

Word Bank

cinturón	botas	camisa
guantes	calcetines	sombrero
chaqueta	falda	zapatos
pantalones	vestido	

¹zapotos
ᶠf ²p ³a ⁴n
³calcetines
h a l ⁵c ⁶b
a d a vestido
q a l n t
u ⁸guantes t a
e e u s
t ⁹sombrero
¹⁰camisa n
ó

42

Matching Clothes

At the bottom of each picture, write the English word that matches the Spanish and the pictures. Write the Spanish words next to the English at the bottom of the page.

falda	zapatos	pantalones cortos	cinturón
skirt	shoes	shorts	belt
abrigo	calcetines	vestido	botas
coat	socks	dress	boots
guantes	pantalones	chaqueta	blusa
gloves	pants	jacket	blouse
gorro	sandalias	camisa	
cap	sandals	shirt	

1. skirt __falda__
2. belt __cinturón__
3. jacket __chaqueta__
4. socks __calcetines__
5. coat __abrigo__
6. shirt __camisa__
7. sandals __sandalias__
8. dress __vestido__
9. cap __gorro__
10. pants __pantalones__
11. gloves __guantes__
12. boots __botas__
13. shoes __zapatos__
14. blouse __blusa__
15. shorts __pantalones cortos__

43

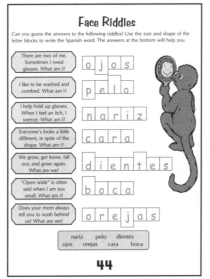

Face Riddles

Can you guess the answers to the following riddles? Use the size and shape of the letter blocks to write the Spanish word. The answers at the bottom will help you.

There are two of me. Sometimes I need glasses. What am I?	ojos
I like to be washed and combed. What am I?	pelo
I help hold up glasses. When I feel an itch, I sneeze. What am I?	nariz
Everyone's looks a little different, in spite of the shape. What am I?	cara
We grow, get loose, fall out, and grow again. What are we?	dientes
"Open wide" is often said when I am too small. What am I?	boca
Does your mom always tell you to wash behind us? What are we?	orejas

nariz pelo dientes
ojos orejas cara boca

44

A Blank Face

Fill in the blanks with the missing letters. Use the Spanish words below to help you.

d
i
P e n boca
e t o n
l e j a
o r e j a s r
s i
z

nariz	pelo	dientes	ojos	orejas	cara	boca

Which word didn't you use? __cara__

Color each block that has a letter k inside. Do not color the blocks with numbers. What hidden word did you find? __boca__

45

77

How Are You?

Label each facial feature with a Spanish word from the Word Bank.

Word Bank
cara
ojos
boca
nariz
pelo
dientes
orejas

pelo — nariz — cara

dientes — ojos — boca — orejas

Copy the Spanish word that matches each face pictured.

happy — alegre — alegre
sad — triste — triste
crying — llorando — llorando

smiling — sonriendo — sonriendo
angry — enojado — enojado
thinking — pensando — pensando

46

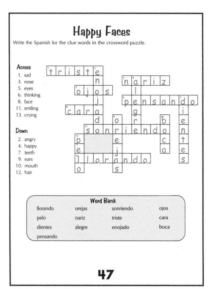

Happy Faces

Write the Spanish for the clue words in the crossword puzzle.

Across
1. sad
3. nose
5. eyes
6. thinking
8. face
11. smiling
13. crying

Down
2. angry
4. happy
7. teeth
9. ears
10. mouth
12. hair

triste
nariz
ojos
pensando
cara
sonriendo
llorando

Word Bank

llorando	orejas	ojos
pelo	nariz	triste
dientes	alegre	cara
pensando	enojado	boca

47

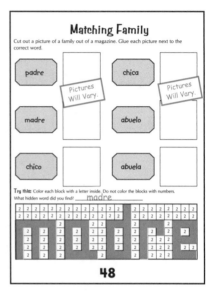

Matching Family

Cut out a picture of a family out of a magazine. Glue each picture next to the correct word.

padre — Pictures Will Vary.

chica — Pictures Will Vary.

madre

abuelo

chico

abuela

Try this: Color each block with a letter inside. Do not color the blocks with numbers. What hidden word did you find? __madre__

48

Family Ties

In each box, copy the Spanish word for family members.

la familia — la familia (family)	el hermano — el hermano (brother)
el padre — el padre (father)	la hermana — la hermana (sister)
la madre — la madre (mother)	el tío — el tío (uncle)
el hijo — el hijo (son)	la tía — la tía (aunt)
la hija — la hija (daughter)	el abuelo — el abuelo (grandfather)
los primos — los primos (cousins)	la abuela — la abuela (grandmother)

Write the Spanish words from above next to the English words.

sister la hermana family la familia father el padre
grandfather el abuelo cousins los primos mother la madre
grandmother la abuela brother el hermano daughter la hija
uncle el tío aunt la tía son el hijo

49

My Family

Write the Spanish word for each clue in the crossword puzzle.

Across
2. son
3. aunt
5. sister
7. grandmother
8. brother
10. cousins

Down
1. mother
2. daughter
4. family
6. grandfather
9. uncle
10. father

tía
hermana
abuela
hermano
primos
madre
hijo

Word Bank

familia	hermano	hijo	tía
primos	madre	tío	abuelo
padre	hermana	hija	abuela

50

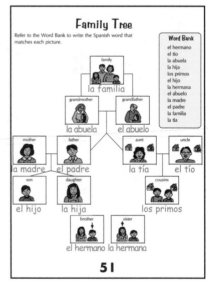

Family Tree

Refer to the Word Bank to write the Spanish word that matches each picture.

Word Bank
el hermano
el tío
la abuela
la hija
los primos
el hijo
la hermana
el abuelo
la madre
el padre
la familia
la tía

family — la familia

grandmother — la abuela grandfather — el abuelo

mother — la madre father — el padre aunt — la tía uncle — el tío

son — el hijo daughter — la hija cousins — los primos

brother — el hermano sister — la hermana

51

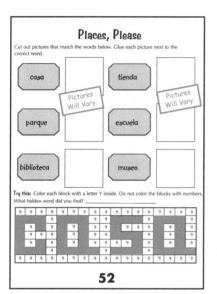

Places, Please

Cut out pictures that match the words below. Glue each picture next to the correct word.

casa   tienda

Pictures Will Vary.   Pictures Will Vary.

parque   escuela

biblioteca   museo

Try this: Color each block with a letter Y inside. Do not color the blocks with numbers. What hidden word did you find? _____

52

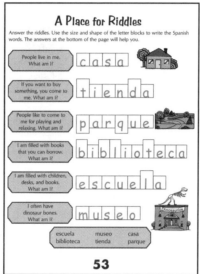

A Place for Riddles

Answer the riddles. Use the size and shape of the letter blocks to write the Spanish words. The answers at the bottom of the page will help you.

People live in me. What am I? — c a s a

If you want to buy something, you come to me. What am I? — t i e n d a

People like to come to me for playing and relaxing. What am I? — p a r q u e

I am filled with books that you can borrow. What am I? — b i b l i o t e c a

I am filled with children, desks, and books. What am I? — e s c u e l a

I often have dinosaur bones. What am I? — m u s e o

escuela   museo   casa
biblioteca   tienda   parque

53

Where Am I?

Refer to the Word Bank and write the Spanish for each place in the community pictured.

cine	museo
granja	zoológico
iglesia	biblioteca
parque	tienda
apartamento	casa
restaurante	escuela

escuela   granja   biblioteca   tienda
museo   casa   apartamento   zoológico
iglesia   restaurante   cine   parque

54

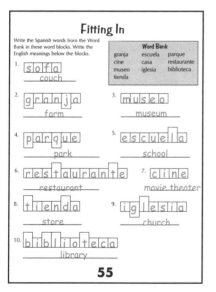

Fitting In

Write the Spanish words from the Word Bank in these word blocks. Write the English meanings below the blocks.

Word Bank
granja   escuela   parque
cine   casa   restaurante
museo   iglesia   biblioteca
tienda

1. s o f a
couch

2. g r a n j a
farm

3. m u s e o
museum

4. p a r q u e
park

5. e s c u e l a
school

6. r e s t a u r a n t e
restaurant

7. c i n e
movie theater

8. t i e n d a
store

9. i g l e s i a
church

10. b i b l i o t e c a
library

55

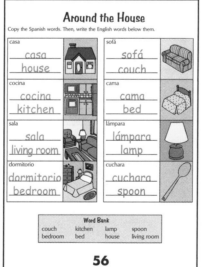

Around the House

Copy the Spanish words. Then, write the English words below them.

casa — casa / house

sofá — sofá / couch

cocina — cocina / kitchen

cama — cama / bed

sala — sala / living room

lámpara — lámpara / lamp

dormitorio — dormitorio / bedroom

cuchara — cuchara / spoon

Word Bank
couch   kitchen   lamp   spoon
bedroom   bed   house   living room

56

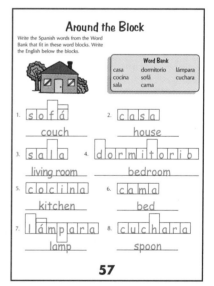

Around the Block

Write the Spanish words from the Word Bank that fit in these word blocks. Write the English below the blocks.

Word Bank
casa   dormitorio   lámpara
cocina   sofá   cuchara
sala   cama

1. s o f á
couch

2. c a s a
house

3. s a l a
living room

4. d o r m i t o r i b
bedroom

5. c o c i n a
kitchen

6. c a m a
bed

7. l á m p a r a
lamp

8. c u c h a r a
spoon

57

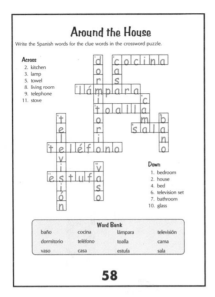

Around the House

Write the Spanish words for the clue words in the crossword puzzle.

Across
2. kitchen
3. lamp
5. towel
8. living room
9. telephone
11. stove

Down
1. bedroom
2. house
4. bed
6. television set
7. bathroom
10. glass

Crossword answers:
- d o r m i t o r i o (down)
- c o c i n a
- c a s a
- l á m p a r a
- t o a l l a
- c a m b o
- s a l a
- t e l e v i s i ó n
- t e l é f o n o
- e s t u f a
- v a s o
- b a ñ o

Word Bank			
baño	cocina	lámpara	televisión
dormitorio	teléfono	toalla	cama
vaso	casa	estufa	sala

58

Match Words and Pictures

Cut out pictures from a magazine and glue each picture next to the correct word.

silla

borrador

mesa

Pictures Will Vary.

lápiz

tijeras

libro

59

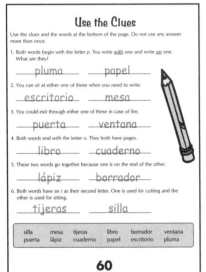

Use the Clues

Use the clues and the words at the bottom of the page. Do not use any answer more than once.

1. Both words begin with the letter *p*. You write <u>with</u> one and write <u>on</u> one. What are they?

   pluma   papel

2. You can sit at either one of these when you need to write.

   escritorio   mesa

3. You could exit through either one of these in case of fire.

   puerta   ventana

4. Both words end with the letter *o*. They both have pages.

   libro   cuaderno

5. These two words go together because one is on the end of the other.

   lápiz   borrador

6. Both words have an *i* as their second letter. One is used for cutting and the other is used for sitting.

   tijeras   silla

silla	mesa	tijeras	libro	borrador	ventana
puerta	lápiz	cuaderno	papel	escritorio	pluma

60

Around the Room

In each box, copy the Spanish word for the classroom object pictured.

silla	silla	mesa	mesa
puerta	puerta	pluma	pluma
ventana	ventana	borrador	borrador
lápiz	lápiz	cuaderno	cuaderno
papel	papel	libro	libro
escritorio	escritorio	tijeras	tijeras

Write the Spanish words from above next to the English words.

window ventana chair silla table mesa
eraser borrador scissors tijeras door puerta
desk escritorio pen pluma notebook cuaderno
paper papel book libro pencil lápiz

61

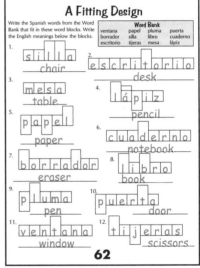

A Fitting Design

Write the Spanish words from the Word Bank that fit in these word blocks. Write the English meanings below the blocks.

Word Bank			
ventana	papel	pluma	puerta
borrador	silla	libro	cuaderno
escritorio	tijeras	mesa	lápiz

1. s i l l a — chair
2. e s c r i t o r i o — desk
3. m e s a — table
4. l á p i z — pencil
5. p a p e l — paper
6. c u a d e r n o — notebook
7. b o r r a d o r — eraser
8. l i b r o — book
9. p l u m a — pen
10. p u e r t a — door
11. v e n t a n a — window
12. t i j e r a s — scissors

62

Classroom Clutter

Draw a picture to illustrate each of the Spanish words. Refer to the Word Bank at the bottom of the page to help you.

Pictures Will Vary.

silla	ventana
mesa	puerta
tijeras	papel
libro	cuaderno
lápiz	escritorio
borrador	pluma

Word Bank				
eraser	door	scissors	pen	window	paper
chair	notebook	pencil	desk	book	table

63

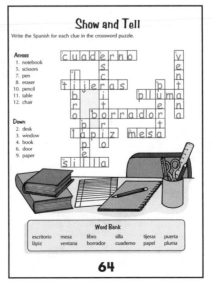

Show and Tell

Write the Spanish for each clue in the crossword puzzle.

Across
1. notebook
5. scissors
7. pen
8. eraser
10. pencil
11. table
12. chair

Down
2. desk
3. window
4. book
6. door
9. paper

Crossword answers:
- c u a d e r n o
- v e n t a n a
- e s c r i t o r i o
- t i j e r a s
- l i b r o
- p l u m a
- p u e r t a
- b o r r a d o r
- l á p i z
- m e s a
- s i l l a

Word Bank					
escritorio	mesa	libro	silla	tijeras	puerta
lápiz	ventana	borrador	cuaderno	papel	pluma

64